W9-BNW-245

137 cn
CYT 'conclusion'
+ CT on white

The One and the Many in the
Canterbury Tales

The One and the Many

in the

Canterbury Tales

TRAUGOTT LAWLER

1980

Archon Books

© Traugott Lawler 1980

First published 1980 as an Archon Book,

an imprint of The Shoe String Press, Inc.,

Hamden, Connecticut 06514

Library of Congress Cataloging in Publication Data

Lawler, Traugott.
 The one and the many in the Canterbury tales.

 Bibliography: p. 175
 Includes index.
 1. Chaucer, Geoffrey, d. 1400. Canterbury tales.
2. Chaucer, Geoffrey, d. 1400—Philosophy. I. Chaucer,
Geoffrey, d. 1400. Canterbury tales. II. Title.
PR1875.P5L3 1980   821'.1   80-12715
ISBN 0-208-01842-5

for Peter, Dan, Kate, *and* Greg

Contents

Acknowledgments

My major debt is to two large groups of people: the scholars and critics who have written on Chaucer's poetry before me, and whose value to me is far greater than my relatively sparse footnoting may suggest; and the students at Yale and Northwestern whose stimulating questions, arguments, and discussion have helped me clarify my ideas about the *Canterbury Tales.*

I am grateful to the American Council of Learned Societies for awarding me a fellowship for the year 1977-78; the encouragement it implied was worth almost as much as the time. My gratitude extends also to the several scholars who supported my application, and whom I have thanked personally.

Leonard Barkan, Ralph Hanna, Frank McConnell, and Martin Mueller did me the dual kindness of both listening and answering back, as did Karen Mouscher and Sigrid Perry. To Stephen Barney I owe the largest debt of all; he read my entire draft with great care and made numerous penetrating and helpful criticisms.

I wish also to record my enduring gratitude to Father Thomas Grace, S. J., under whose guidance I first studied Chaucer. I wish he were alive to read this book; I have tried to reach a standard that would not have displeased him.

Evanston, Illinois   TRAUGOTT LAWLER
August 1979

Note on Citations
from the *Canterbury Tales*

The edition cited is Robert A. Pratt, *The Tales of Canterbury* (Boston: Houghton Mifflin, 1974). All italics are mine, except words in French and Latin. Citations are by group letter and line number (e.g., A3740), except that in chapter 7 the Parson's Tale is cited by line number only; when appropriate the title of the tale is added, in the standard abbreviated form as listed in F. N. Robinson's *Works of Geoffrey Chaucer,* 2d ed. (Boston: Houghton Mifflin, 1957), p. 647 (add WBP for Wife of Bath's Prologue). In citations of more than one line, only the number of the last line is given. I have regularly used the phrase "the poem," despite its inaccuracy, to refer to the *Canterbury Tales* as a whole.

1. Introduction

In the Knight's Tale, as Palamon and Arcite and their retinues
gather in Athens for the tournament to see who will win
Emelye, we see

> The paleys ful of peple up and doun,
> Heere thre, ther ten, holdynge hir questioun,
> Dyvynynge of thise Thebane knyghtes two.
> Somme seyden thus, somme seyde, "It shal be so";
> Somme helden with hym with the blake berd,
> Somme with the balled, somme with the thikke herd;
> Somme seyde he looked grymme, and he wolde
>   fighte:—
> "He hath a sparth of twenty pound of wighte."
> Thus was the halle ful of divynynge.   (A2521)

Despite the statement at the start that people's guesses refer
to Palamon and Arcite ("thise Thebane knyghtes two"), the
opinions offered in fact cover a wider ground. "Hym with the
blake berd" is Lygurge, Palamon's chief hero. The bald man
is some unnamed knight, as is probably the thick-haired man
(Lygurge's hair is "longe" [A2143], Emetrius's "crispe"
[A2165]; Palamon's and Arcite's hair is not described). The
three "he's" in ll. 2519-20 are probably three more unnamed
knights of the two hundred Palamon and Arcite have
brought. The "thus" and "so" of l. 2516 are two contradictory

11

opinions, purposely left unspecified. The passage not only emphasizes differences of opinion; it covers many speakers, and the speakers speak of many subjects. It need not have: since every knight is either on Palamon's side or Arcite's, every opinion expressed must in fact favor either one or the other. But Chaucer obscures that simple dichotomy, not only by reporting opinions about various unknown subordinate knights rather than about the two principals, but also by leaving the identifications obscure. Except for Lygurge, we do not know which side any knight mentioned is on. Altogether, the passage succeeds in rendering the impression of a very wide diversity of opinion.[1]

It is quite a typical passage in the *Canterbury Tales*. In the Squire's Tale, a lengthy passage (F189-224) describes the diversity of opinions about how the magic horse "koude go, and was of bras."

> Diverse folk diversely han demed;
> As many heddes, as many wittes ther been.
> They murmured as dooth a swarm of been,
> And maden skiles after hir fantasies.
> . . . .
> Of sondry doutes thus they jangle and trete,
> As lewed peple demeth comunly
> Of thynges that been maad moore subtilly
> Than they kan in hir lewednesse comprehende;
> They demen gladly to the badder ende.   (F205, 224)

When the Canon's pot bursts in the first part of the Canon's Yeoman's Tale, each of the Canon's accomplices suggests a different cause:

> Every man chit, and halt hym yvele apayd.
> Somme seyde it was long on the fir makyng;
> Somme seyde nay, it was on the blowyng—
> Thanne was I fered, for that was myn office.
> "Straw!" quod the thridde, "ye been lewed and nyce.

It was nat tempred as it oghte be."
"Nay," quod the fourthe, "stynt and herkne me.
By cause oure fyr was nat maad of beech,
That is the cause, and oother noon, so theech!"
I kan nat telle wheron it was long,
But wel I woot greet strif is us among.   (G931)

In the Man of Law's Tale, when the Sultan calls his privy
council to advise him how to have Custance, "Diverse men
diverse thynges seyden" (B211). In the Merchant's Tale, when
January asks his friends to ratify his decision to marry,

Diverse men diversely hym tolde
Of mariage manye ensamples olde.
Somme blamed it, somme preised it, certeyn. (E1471)

When the Miller completes his tale, "Diverse folk diversely
they seyde" (A3857). When the knight in the Wife of Bath's
Tale sets out to discover what women love most,

he ne koude arryven in no coost
Wher as he myghte fynde in this matere
Two creatures accordynge in-feere.
Somme seyde wommen loven best richesse,
Somme seyde honour, somme seyde jolynesse. . . .
(D926)

It should be noted that since no two creatures agree,
"somme" here, as in the passage from the Canon's Yeoman's
Tale, means "one," not "some"; the separation is complete:
everyone has his own opinion.

In all these cases, the diversity is eventually resolved into,
or contrasted with, some unity—though that unity is itself
usually in some way precarious, threatened, or incomplete.
The passage in the Knight's Tale is followed immediately by
a particularly grand appearance of Theseus, alone, "at a
wyndow set, / Arrayed right as he were a god in trone," who

silences the crowd with the help of a herald who cries
"Oo!"—his very cry means "one." Theseus then sets a series of
limitations on the tournament. Of course he too is still in
doubt about the outcome; the diversity of possibilities about
which the people "divine" is settled not by Theseus but by
time—though still dubiously, since there seem to be two
winners. The ultimate unity set against this diversity is Theseus's final harmonious vision of the whole complex of events
and values in the tale.

The passage in the Squire's Tale (which continues with
further diverse wondering about the other gifts) is followed
first by a grand entrance of Cambyuskan and then by the
knight's authoritative explanation of how the horse works.
The conflict in the Canon's Yeoman's Tale is silenced by the
Canon, though only briefly; its more effective counterpart is
first the Yeoman's clear implication that *all* experiments end
in failure and quarreling, so that the diversity of opinion is
enclosed within a weary sense of sameness, and then his
decisive dismissal of the whole science of alchemy, as practiced by the Canon, as inconclusive. The Sultan's council
finally agrees he should be christened and marry Custance
(though his mother has other ideas); the diversity of advice
offered January is quickly reduced to the debate between
Justinus and Placebo, and January single-mindedly chooses
Placebo's point of view. Here, too, ambiguities abound: the
Merchant's Tale is pervaded by duplicity, and unlike the
Knight's Tale does not reach harmony at any level. The
diverse response to the Miller's Tale is contained by the
general pleasure, from which only the Reeve stands apart.
And the old woman in the Wife of Bath's Tale provides the
knight with an answer to which all assent; furthermore, she
reinforces the unifying impulse with ultimate thoroughness
when she first marries the knight, then resolves his dilemma,
and her own ambivalent nature, at the end of the tale. Yet
here too the unity achieved is open to doubt, since it is
evidently a function of the unique, and therefore controversial or divergent, notions proper to the teller of the tale.

14

The subject of this book is the subject which these brief passages illustrate: the complementary relationship in the *Canterbury Tales* between unity and diversity, oneness and multiplicity—between the one and the many. I shall argue that this relationship is the most pervasive issue in the poem, and its major unifying force. And the argument that the poem is unified implies the further argument that Chaucer, though he grants value both to unity and to diversity, and though he finds unity difficult to achieve, ultimately places a higher value on unity. I have tried, however, not to produce a "thesis-ridden" book, or to engage continually in abstractions; I use the relationship of one to many less as a thesis than as a focus and springboard for discussion; it is not so much the thesis itself as the various interpretations and small syntheses it generates that are the center of the book. I have tried to provide an organizing rubric for certain related phenomena in the *Canterbury Tales*, not a key to Chaucer's mind.

That the opposition of one and many is central to the poem is evident both in its subject and its form. Its subject is "a compaignye / of sondry folk," a group of separate, individual people whom we see asunder, that is, in their private identity, but also in company, that is, comprising a group that has its own "higher" identity. Nor is the company of pilgrims the only group to which each individual pilgrim belongs. Each is strongly, indeed primarily, identified with his profession, and as we read the General Prologue we are forced to notice how many general, unifying categories lie just beneath their individuality: not only profession but sex, social class, family, lay or religious status, wealth, dress, and many others. The form of the poem invites consideration of the relationship of many to one in several ways: first, in that it is a single poem which comprises a series of separate tales; second, in that the tales are further grouped into smaller units—the "Groups" or "Fragments"—and are susceptible as well of other groupings by theme or genre, which form an intermediate level of unity or generality; and finally in that each particular tale bears a relationship to the "general" prologue.

The One and the Many

The opening sentence of the poem illustrates immediately the intricate relation of general (one) and particular (many). Its movement from the general to the particular, continued in the second sentence, is recognized by all readers. But it is less well recognized how much emphasis on the general remains despite that movement. The sentence implies the following generalities:

a. that one April is like another;
b. that there are various general levels of being: planets, plants, animals, people; and that within each genus, one individual is like another;
c. that all these respond to spring, each in its "generic" way;
d. that these responses constitute an ascending order of value or interest;
e. that there is a standard human April activity (as in the pictures that accompany the months in Books of Hours).

Despite the move from general to particular (which does not occur until "and specially" in l. 15), and despite the implicit ascending order of value, the chief stress is on the general, on common, unifying features. The sentence honors men by giving them the final, climactic place; but it also humbles them by insisting that they share common traits with animals and plants. It makes, to be sure, certain distinctions between men and other beings. Men "longen," for example, before they "wende"; birds merely sing, without forethought or conscious desire. Plants are objects of verbs, or the subjects of passive verbs: "Aprill . . . hath . . . bathed every veyne," "engendred is the flour," "Zephirus . . . inspired hath . . . the tendre croppes." Birds act on their own ("maken melodye"), but are also acted upon ("so priketh hem Nature"); only men are strictly subjects: they long, they wend—and yet they too are the object of an influence, albeit supernatural and personal, for Saint Thomas "hem hath holpen." Yet these distinctions are all contained within one sentence: the syntax holds the diversity within a larger unity. We are made aware of both the diversity and the unity, of individuating distinctions and common features, of progression and stasis, all existing simultaneously in harmonious balance. If there is a movement toward the particular, there is also a pull toward the general; and the syntactic unity suggests a preference for the one. One expects, perhaps, that some similar balance and preference will be sought in the entire poem, though it may be more difficult of attainment.

A second random example of the issue is two lines from the Wife of Bath's Prologue. She says of St. Paul that "He wolde that every wight were swich as he" (D81), that is, a virgin; but she claims in opposition (quoting, in fact, Paul's own qualification to the first statement, but not acknowledging that) that "everich hath of God a propre yifte" (D103). Here the contrast of one and many is put in terms of the ideal and the real. The ideal, Paul's wish, is that everybody should be the same, all virgins, and thus "one" in two senses: having a common identity, and all single, i.e., unmarried. In fact, people differ: reality is multiple. And since the Wife's "propre yifte" is to be a wife, there is a further implication of multiplicity: one does not remain single but copulates, the result of which is to "wexe and multiplye," which "God bad us" (D28). The Wife sets Paul and God against each other, disunites them. Of course marriage is itself ideally a unity, a joining of many into one, but here and in most places in the poem the partners to a marriage remain partial, and copulation is a mere parody of true unity, "the beast with two backs." Furthermore, multiplicity seems to be sanctioned by God: "proper gifts" are from him, he ordered multiplication. Yet oneness has its own authority in St. Paul; at their deepest level of opposition, the lines suggest that authority itself is diverse and contradictory—an issue explored by Chaucer most directly in the Nuns' Priest's Tale.[2] Finally, if we consult the original single, balanced sentence in St. Paul, "Volo enim omnes vos esse sicut meipsum; sed unusquisque proprium

The One and the Many

donum habet ex Deo" (1 Cor. 7:7), we realize that the true author of these multiplicities is the Wife herself, dividing the sentence and exploiting it for her own, quite remarkably individual purposes. More generally, the lines are one manifestation of a constant issue, a major intellectual motive in the poem: how far are people like each other, how far unique? They also touch on the general theme of multiplicity. The Wife multiplies husbands; the Pardoner likewise multiplies his income by inducing others to believe his bones will multiply theirs; the Canon struggles to multiply gold. The fiend in the Friar's Tale says he can take multiple shapes; the tercelet in the Squire's Tale is "ful of doublenesse"; the friar in the Summoner's Tale is vexed, amusingly, by division. All would be better off if they accepted unity; although those who do, who are "sad" or "alwey oon" like Grisilde or Custance, as a guard against the multiple vicissitudes of this inconstant life, meet their own sort of difficulty.

Let us consider next the arrival at Athens of Palamon and Arcite with their retinues, not long before the passage with which our discussion began. Each single knight instead of fighting alone in the woods is now at the head of a company of one hundred knights. This is a multiplication whose aim is to integrate. Students reading the Knight's Tale for the first time often complain that Theseus has foolishly "escalated" the quarrel; but clearly his intention is to transform an isolated and unlawful vendetta into a legitimate communal ritual, to return Palamon and Arcite to the community, to impose a centripetal force on their quarrel (which has come about because they have discovered a breach in their oath of unity, or perhaps because they have discovered that love is a more multiple and divisive phenomenon than they once thought). From the tournament a single winner will emerge (or so Theseus thinks).

At the same time, the reader of the *Canterbury Tales* may perceive a still further level of integration. For the gathering of the combatants has striking parallels with the gathering, so recently described, of pilgrims at Southwark. Here again we

18

have a "compaignye," described both in general and in
selective individual portraits (of Lygurge and Emetrius)
which emphasize clothing, come together in a certain place at
a certain time (cf. "at nyght" [A23], "aboute pryme" [A2189]);
and again the account focuses eventually on the host, here
Theseus, and the "ease" with which he accomodates them, on
some details of their communal meal, and, at the end, on
what happened early the next morning: "The Sonday nyght,
er day bigan to sprynge" (A2209; cf. A822), Palamon "roos to
wenden on his pilgrymage" to the shrine of the "blisful"
Venus (A2214, 2215). Eventually Theseus (through his herald)
proposes the rules of the contest.

Especially striking is the parallel between Theseus and the
Host:

Greet cheere made oure Hoost us everichon,
And to the soper sette he us anon.
He served us with vitaille at the beste. (A749)

This Theseus, this duc, this worthy knyght,
Whan he had broght hem into his citee,
And inned hem, everich at his degree,
He festeth hem, and dooth so greet labour
To esen hem and doon hem al honour,
That yet men wenen that no mannes wit
Of noon estaat ne koude amenden it. (A2196)

Besides the "inning" and feasting, one notes the effort "to
esen hem" (cf. "wel we weren esed" [A29], "and of a myrthe I
am right now bythoght, / To doon yow ese" [A768]), and—
echoing the General Prologue somewhat more largely—the
concern for degree and the eagerness of the narrator to
render superlative praise. In the General Prologue the superlative mode is applied both to the Host ("a fairer burgeys was
ther noon in Chepe / . . . of manhod hym lakkede right
naught" [A756]), and (besides to many other individuals) to
the company as a whole: the Host claims not to have seen

19

The One and the Many

"this yeer so myrie a compaignye / Atones in this herberwe as is now" (A765). Theseus's company is likewise exceptional:

> And sikerly ther trowed many a man
> That nevere, sithen that the world bigan,
> As for to speke of knyghthod of hir hond,
> As fer as God hath maked see and lond,
> Nas of so fewe so noble a compaignye.   (A2105)

The Knight actually raises explicitly the idea of Englishmen gathering:

> For if ther fille tomorwe swich a cas,
> Ye knowen wel that every lusty knyght
> That loveth paramours and hath his myght,
> Were it in Engelond or elleswhere,
> They wolde, hir thankes, wilnen to be there.   (A2114)

What are we to make of these parallels? To suppose that the Knight is offering a subtle compliment to the Host, or an echo of their experience to the pilgrims, would be absurd. Nor is it at all likely that Chaucer had any specific parallel in mind. What we have here rather is something like what is called a "theme" in oral-formulaic poetry: Chaucer—or medieval poetry at large—had developed a conventional way of describing the gathering of a fellowship for a formal, conventional event, and he makes use of it here as well as in the General Prologue. (Many of the details—the superlative mode, some portraiture, the emphasis on hospitality—appear again in the account of Walter's mock second "wedding" in the Clerk's Tale.) But this very conventionalism is a unifying force: the parallel details make us see that a gathering of knights for a tournament and a gathering of pilgrims for a pilgrimage are not wholly distinct events. Furthermore, the orderly integration, the establishment of one winner, that Theseus hopes to accomplish through the tournament, is foiled by Arcite's accidental death: the tournament creates

20

more disorder than Theseus bargained for. Similarly, as the pilgrimage progresses we witness significant breakdowns both in the sense of orderly community the General Prologue presents and in the Host's orderly plan for the storytelling contest. The passage makes us reflect finally, not so much on the similarities of fellowships, but on the similarity of the Host and Theseus—and perhaps Chaucer—as figures of authority, programmatic planners of unity. Such patterns of repetition, frequent in the poem, probe deeply into the question of the relationship of one and many.

A final brief example is Chaucer's preface to *Melibee:*

It is a moral tale vertuous,
Al be it told somtyme in sondry wyse
Of sondry folk, as I shal yow devyse.
As thus: ye woot that every Evaungelist,
That telleth us the peyne of Jhesu Crist,
Ne seith nat alle thyng as his felawe dooth;
But nathelees hir sentence is al sooth.
And alle acorden as in hire sentence,
Al be ther in hir tellyng difference.
For somme of hem seyn moore, and somme seyn lesse,
Whan they his pitous passioun expresse—
I meene of Mark, Mathew, Luk, and John—
But doutelees hir sentence is al oon.
Therfore, lordynges alle, I yow biseche,
If that yow thynke I varie as in my speche,
As thus, though that I telle somwhat moore
Of proverbes than ye han herd bifoore
Comprehended in this litel tretys heere,
To enforce with th'effect of my mateere;
And though I nat the same wordes seye
As ye han herd, yet to yow alle I preye
Blameth me nat; for, as in my sentence,
Shul ye nowher fynden difference
Fro the sentence of this tretys lite
After the which this murye tale I write.   (B964)

The One and the Many

This passage describes a double relationship of one to many. It says that the four Gospels are one in the "sentence" of their account of Christ's passion, and it says that Chaucer's *Melibee* and one or more previous versions of it are also one in "sentence." (Indeed, the whole controversial subject of "sentence" and "words," of "fruit and chaff," of "kernel and shell," is a particular manifestation of the larger issue of the relation of one to many.) Furthermore, the pair of instances combine to imply a "higher generalization": that in general in literature several versions of the same essential story may exist. But Chaucer avoids stating this generalization, and avoids the still higher generalization, that all stories are the same story. In each of the two separate instances, that is, in the Gospels and in the story of Melibee, he is willing to emphasize unity, to say that variations are negligible; but in the combined instance, though he sees a common feature, he allows the differences to remain undisturbed.

I stress this point because of the notion some hold that all medieval literature promotes charity, and because D. W. Robertson, who holds it most tenaciously, has used this passage to argue that all the *Canterbury Tales* have the same sentence.[3] If Chaucer really held that all literature had the same sentence, he could have pointed out that the sentence of the Gospels and that of *Melibee* are one: both insist centrally on forgiveness. The fact that he does not, that he holds the Gospels to the status of a simile, suggests that Chaucer, though he is anxious to perceive unity amid diversity, is also anxious to let differences stand. He wishes not to efface, ignore, or depreciate particulars and surfaces, but only to discern a balance between them and such unity as lies behind or beneath them. Two other aspects of this passage are instructive. One is that though particular differences (the many) may not affect the "sentence," they have some value: Chaucer has chosen to add proverbs (indeed, many, many proverbs) "to enforce with th'effect." The second, a reinforcement of my earlier point, is that the passage does not provide license for supposing that any multiplicity of very different things is capable of being subsumed under some unifying "sentence." The gospels all "his pitous passioun expresse": they treat the same event, Christ's passion, and all make it appear "pitous." They vary in saying more or less; each "ne seith nat alle thyng as his felawe dooth." Chaucer's *Melibee* differs from versions "ye han herd bifoore" in the addition of some proverbs and in not employing "the same wordes." The passage implies that an inner unity can be discerned beneath a surface of multiplicity, but only when that multiplicity is trivial and limited. It certainly gives no basis for holding that all the tales in the poem have the same sentence. It is instructive for its moderation, for its untroubled acceptance of multiplicity as well as for its insistence on unity. It is notable too in associating the subject with authorship, since, as I shall argue, authority is one of the major representatives in the poem of the one.

The relationship of one and many is evident also in the plots and themes of many tales. *Melibee* is a good example. Melibee responds to the attack on his honor by calling a council of all his friends. These quickly reach a general agreement that he should make war, although as usual diverse folk speak diversely. A lawyer suggests moderation, but "the mooste partie of that compaignye han scorned this olde wise man" (B2225); another old wise man is shouted down by "wel ny alle atones" (B2233). Prudence then persuades Melibee that "the trouthe of thynges and the profit ben rather founde in fewe folk that ben wise and ful of reson, than by gret multitude of folk ther every man crieth and clatereth what that hym liketh. Soothly swich multitude is nat honest" (B2259). Eventually Melibee eschews the many, despite their near unanimity, for the counsel of Prudence alone. The movement of the tale, furthermore, is from diversity to unity. Melibee begins at odds with Prudence and with his enemies, and his counselors, though at first united, soon become at odds with each other. In the course of the tale Melibee becomes united with Prudence and then with his enemies, and his counselors come to agree with him and with each other. The tale demonstrates that "oon of the gretteste and moost sovereyn thyng that is in this world is unitee and pees" (B2868). This unity is achieved by subordination of individuality; a similar movement occurs in the tales of the Knight, Franklin, Clerk, and Parson, and in the Wife of Bath's Prologue and Tale.

The Monk's Tale is a kind of parody of the issue of one and many: his many tales all with the same sentence suggest that unity is dull. Furthermore, the Monk's characters are, typically, loners who suffer disintegration. The issue is parodied more amusingly in the Miller's Tale, the Wife's Prologue, the Merchant's Tale, and elsewhere when one woman has many lovers, and conversely in the Wife's Tale and the Nuns' Priest's Tale when a single male is surrounded by females. In the Summoner's Tale, the friar fails to live up to the ideals of brotherhood that his calling requires: he is out for number one. Yet ironically, since the Summoner implies that all friars are similarly selfish and hypocritical, there is unity among the brotherhood after all. The friar expresses his selfishness by warning Thomas against dividing his donations among "diverse freres":

Lo, ech thyng that is oned in himselve
Is moore strong than whan it is toscatered.   (D1969)

The squire's plan for dividing the fart equally among the members of the friar's convent indicates that the friars have achieved unity only in empty and corrupt ways. Virtually all the tales make their contribution to this complex issue. This fact is itself an aspect of the issue; and meantime the pilgrims in their "group dynamics" enact further manifestations of it.

The major source of diversity in the poem is sex. The major source of unity is order. The relation between the two, though not immediately obvious, is strong. P. M. Kean has described it well:

Order partakes of the nature of the One, perfect, stable,

eternal, and is therefore directly ruled over by God. Disorder, on the other hand, partakes of the nature of multiplicity, instability and impermanence—all characteristics of the created world below the moon, which becomes more and more imperfect the further it is removed from the One from which it takes its being. The world below the moon is subject to Fortune and, in close association with Fortune, to the planets. These have power delegated to them from the One, as does Nature. Nature symbolizes the divine purpose of achieving a modicum of order out of the disorder of the world, so far removed from the perfection from which it originally sprang. But it is the very perfection of the originating One which ensures the infinite variety of Nature. Nature, therefore, while she works for order, also works with Venus, natural sexual passion, to bring about the continued propagation of the whole gamut of creatures. In the case of mankind, however, Venus all too often goes astray, divorces herself from Nature and nullifies her plan by making passion barren. Man, in fact, occupies a key position in the world of change. On the one hand, he can spoil the order which the divine plan is always working to introduce into its multiplicity. On the other, because, unlike any other creature, he is made in the image of the One, he has a potential for order far beyond any other of Nature's charges. If man is considered from the point of view of this key position in the natural world, marriage becomes the point at which he is able to exert the greatest force in either direction—for order or disorder.[4]

The Knight's Tale demonstrates the order in the cosmos and in the state (though it acknowledges various chances of disorder). Characteristically, however, Chaucer treats this in sexual terms: order is maintained in both cosmos and state by males, Jupiter and Theseus; Venus and Ypolita are subjugated. The tale begins with the wiping out of the Amazons, who maintain an unnatural state.

This general order ought to be imitated at the particular level of the family, wherein the husband should hold sway, and the wife should be "an help semblable to hymself" (*Melibee*, B2294). "Heere may ye se that if that wommen were nat goode, and hir conseil goode and profitable, oure Lord God of hevene wolde neither han wroght hem, ne called hem help of man, but rather confusioun of man" (B2296). Women should be "semblable" to men; as the Miller says, quoting Cato, "men sholde wedde his simylitude" (A3228):— but they are not similar, they are different. They should help; too often they in fact confuse, i.e., ruin. Women thus represent a double divergence: they fail to be like men, and they perform the opposite function to that ordained for them. Thus despite the general order asserted, and vindicated, in the Knight's Tale, at the level of particular households multiplicity reigns: men and women are unlike. It is this fundamental twoness or failure of unity that provides the impetus for many of the tales: in varying ways for the Miller's Tale, Shipman's Tale, Wife of Bath's Prologue and Tale, Clerk's Tale, Merchant's Tale, Nuns' Priest's Tale, Manciple's Tale. The Nuns' Priest's Tale is particularly rich in this regard because Chauntecleer tries to be a lord like Theseus, a ruler of his state, but is in fact henpecked. Chaucer was deeply aware of cosmic order, and of principles of unity in the cosmos, but also deeply and comically aware of the disorder and disunity on the level of everyday household living. There is a general parallel to this double awareness in the form of the poem, wherein the harmony celebrated in the General Prologue—in which one feels a certain artificial quality, as if it were only the product of the poet's art, or the narrator's appetite for harmony, or the Host's dominance, or the pilgrims' awareness of the need for a sense of community on the pilgrimage—breaks down as the poem develops and the distance at which the characters are held from us lessens.

This is not a study of Chaucer's sources; nevertheless, something should be said about the possible provenance of this issue in Chaucer's mind. Surely he did not set out to write a poem about unity and multiplicity. More likely he set out to write a number of tales, and set them in a frame of pilgrimage; and he found the issue implicit in the form. His interest in it is not dissimilar from that of any thoughtful person, of his time or our own, who seeks to impose meaning on the diverse flow of experience, or who reflects on the complex ways in which persons, things, ideas are at once distinct from and yet allied with other persons, things, and ideas. It is unlikely to have come from extensive reading in philosophy. Yet surely Chaucer knew in general the Platonic and Neoplatonic tradition, particularly as it is expressed by Pythagoras in the last book of Ovid's *Metamorphoses*, and by Saint Paul, Boethius, Alain de Lille, and Jean de Meun. To see how the issue functions in two of these authors, Boethius and Saint Paul, will suffice to suggest that it was a central issue, and that literary models were available to him if he needed them.

Boethius, in the *Consolation of Philosophy*, having given way to various appetites and the "felefolde colours and desceytes of thilke merveylous monstre Fortune," learns from Philosophy to reintegrate his life in the search for "the soverayn good that conteneth in hymself alle maner goodes," or which is "oon and symple in his nature" though "the wikkidnesse of men departeth it and divideth it."[5] Unity derives its value for Boethius, however, from its dynamic interplay with multiplicity: "God disponith in his purveaunce singulerly and stablely the thinges that ben to doone; but he amynistreth in many maneris and in diverse tymes by destyne thilke same thinges that he hath disponyd" (Book 4, prose 6). We see this dynamic interplay especially in the poems, which so frequently celebrate the orderly variety of the universe. Thus, for example, in the famous ninth meter of Book 3, God is praised for forming "the faire world," and commanding "that this world, parfytly ymakid, have frely and absolut his parfyte parties":

Thow . . . enhauncest the soules and the lasse lyves; and,

27

> ablynge hem heye by lyghte waynes or cartes, thow
> sowest hem into hevene and into erthe. And whan thei
> ben convertyd to the by thi benygne lawe, thow makest
> hem retourne ayen to the by ayen-ledynge fyer.

The multitudinous created objects "sowed" into heaven and
earth are accepted as good, and even the very moment of
return to unity with the Creator (for which see the Knight's
Tale, A3037) is envisioned in an image of motion, of shifting
multiplicity, the "ayen-ledynge fyer" *(reduci . . . igne).*
  Unification is a pervasive idea in Paul. He is constantly
striving to preach one gospel, to unify congregations in peace
and love, and in Christ, in whom "all things hold together" in
the famous head-and-body metaphor.[6] Christ stands in relation to the saved as one to many, just as Adam did to sinners
(Rom. 5:15): he has united Jew and Greek, slave and free,
male and female (Gal. 3:28). Paul's great theme of the superiority of faith to law has the preference of one to many as an
implied underpinning. For the law is multiple, a collection of
specific injunctions requiring a discrete knowledge of what
to do in this or that situation or at this or that moment; faith is
one, a simple all-embracing concept that frees. "The whole
law is fulfilled in one word, 'you shall love your neighbor as
yourself'" (Gal. 5:14). The opposition of spirit to flesh is
similar. Ultimately, the spirit is one because it makes for
eternal life, for permanence; the flesh is associated with
death, and death belongs to the many because it is the agent
of change and separation (cf. Gal. 6:8; Rom. 8:6). Paul himself
is single-minded: his life is guided by his memory of one
event, his conversion, and devoted to exploring the significance of one related set of events, the crucifixion and resurrection of Christ. "For I decided to know nothing among you
except Jesus Christ and him crucified" (1 Cor. 2:2).
  Nevertheless, various aspects of multiplicity press constantly against him; like Boethius, he acknowledges the interplay of unity with diversity. His personal experience is varied
and full, as the well-known list of perils in 2 Cor. 11:24-28

witnesses; he has "become all things to all men" (1 Cor. 9:22). The simplification he seeks is not an attempt to deny the fact of multiplicity but to overcome it. Some Christians act as if they had already achieved perfection; they misunderstand that they "are being saved" (1 Cor. 1:18).[7] For process toward a future goal is a central Pauline idea; he constantly insists that unification in Christ, though effected as it were theologically in Christ's death, is a process, not a historically realized event: "I press on toward the goal for the prize of the upward call of God in Christ Jesus" (Phil. 3:14); in Christ the head, "the whole body . . . grows with a growth that is from God" (Col. 2:19). His insistence on process derives from the fact that, filled though he is with the sense of Christ, he remains sharply aware of the forces that multiply and separate, both in individual people and in groups. In himself, he sees the law of sin in his members at war with the law of God in his inmost self; in communities he sees power struggles, contending ideologies, dismay over members who sin.

But above all he is acutely conscious of individuality: "each has his own special gift from God, one of one kind and one of another" (1 Cor. 7:7, the passage the Wife of Bath quotes). He acknowledges again and again the multiplicity of "gifts"—but always hastens to set against it an overarching unity. Thus in 1 Cor. 12, a list of "varieties of gifts" prompts first the comparison to the fact that "all the members of the body, though many, are one body," and then the great thirteenth chapter extolling love. In Rom. 12:4-9 appears the same complex: the body metaphor, the acknowledgment of differing gifts, the exhortation "let love be genuine." In Phil. 2:1-4, individuality is acknowledged in the right to look after one's own interests, but balanced by an injunction against selfishness. In a final "gift" passage, Eph. 4:4-16 (the first verses of which Chaucer paraphrases in the Second Nun's Tale, G207-09), Paul doubly acknowledges multiplicity by associating the idea of variety of gifts with the idea of process—and sets both in the context of the unifying body metaphor: the purpose of multiple gifts is "building up the body of Christ, until we all attain to the unity of the faith. . . . Speaking the truth in love, we are to grow up in every way into him who is the head, into Christ, from whom the whole body, joined and knit together by every joint with which it is supplied, when each part is working properly, makes bodily growth and upbuilds itself in love." Paul's consistent pattern in all these passages is to acknowledge individual differences but to subsume them in a larger vision of unity, usually through the medium of love. The general pattern is remarkably similar to Chaucer's. Again, I do not claim that Chaucer derived his interest in the relation of one to many either from Boethius or Paul; but these authors serve to illustrate the importance of that relationship, and to give some idea of how Chaucer may have seen it applied. His own application of it, appropriately enough, is at once conventional and individual.

My most ambitious hope for this study is that it will provide a single large perspective from which to understand many problems which trouble all readers: not only why the same poem seems susceptible of extremely individualistic and positivistic interpretation on the one hand, and extremely general and programmatic interpretation on the other; but a theoretical framework for Chaucer's interest in stereotypes and classes—especially sexual and professional stereo- types—for the centrality of marriage, for the discrepancies in the plan of the whole and the "fragmentary" status in which Chaucer left the poem, for the purpose and value of *Melibee,* the Parson's Tale, the Retraction, and for the value of the conventional style. My general hope is to improve our under- standing of the wholeness and oneness of the *Canterbury Tales;* but I care for particulars, too, and have striven to put my ideas to the test by applying them to the interpretation of many particular passages. The point of departure for the study proper is an examination of the major role played in the poem by professions, both those of the pilgrims and those of the characters in the tales. Since professionalism has a sexual dimension, this issue moves into that of the opposition of men and women, and the whole subject of marriage. But marriage

Yet we are still on a general level: condition, profession "whiche they weren"), degree, array are categories by which "resoun," equally unsatisfied with the utterly particular as with the merely general, organizes particular details into meaning.[1]

These categories, and others like them, remain very much to the fore in the individual portraits which follow. Concrete, detailed, sharply differentiated though these portraits are, they never wholly submerge one's sense of both this company and the larger human company; they keep us aware of the complex set of relationships with others that places limits on individuality.

Let us take "array," for instance. Faithful to his promise, Chaucer tells us something about what every pilgrim wears except the Cook, the Parson, and the Manciple. Since all wear something different, details about clothing seem particular. Yet generality lurks even here. In the first place, it is not quite true that all wear something different: the guildsmen "were clothed alle in o lyveree / Of a solempne and a greet fraternitee." Clothes can associate as well as differentiate. Furthermore, in most cases the clothing mentioned has a clear appropriateness, either to the profession or to the personal traits of the pilgrim, and often to both, since usually a pilgrim's personal traits are themselves appropriate to his profession. This suggests a general truth, such as "clothes make the man"; it also reinforces professional stereotypes. Thus the Clerk's threadbare jacket fits not only the Clerk's poverty and immateriality but also our standard notion of how intellectuals dress. The Knight's rusty undershirt is only momentarily surprising; since the rust comes from his armor, it signifies his profession, and the studied modesty of it fits the notion of ideal knighthood that the portrait has long since brought to the fore in our minds. The Wife's ample garments signify not only the riches that bought them but the riches that lie beneath them; furthermore, we commonly think of women as caring for clothing. In short, the particularizing value of references to clothing is limited because the refer-

in turn raises the question, as the Wife of Bath saw, of experience and authority, an issue which occupies both my fourth and sixth chapters. The fifth chapter departs from thematic organization to treat the one and the many in terms of the question of how many tales each pilgrim should tell. And since this is related to the question of closure, or the final definition of the poem's nature and contents, the sixth and seventh chapters, though still thematic in their bias, treat specifically the final groups of tales: chapter 6 focuses on the Canon's Yeoman's Tale, a tale whose depth and importance seem to me to have been greatly undervalued, and chapter 7 on the Parson's Tale and the Retraction.

2. Professionalism
the Poem as Fablia

Let us begin our discussion at a point reached but
in the previous chapter: the second sentence o
Though, as I have said, this sentence descends qu
particular, it too has its level of generality:

> At nyght was come into that hostelrye
> Wel nyne and twenty in a compaignye
> Of sondry folk, by aventure yfalle
> In felaweshipe, and pilgrimes were they all
> That toward Caunterbury wolden ryde.

The operative words here are "compaignye," "fel
"alle." Twenty-nine separate individuals, "sondry
prise a company, a general unit. Chance ("aver
transformed their separate arrivals at the hostelry i
unit, transformed them into a fellowship; the gene
ry "pilgrim" now unites them all.

This set of general statements then puts in mot
drive toward the particular. Reason demands it;

> acordaunt to resoun
> To telle yow al the condicioun
> Of ech of hem, so as it semed me,
> And whiche they weren, and of what degree
> And eek in what array that they were inne.

ences regularly perform the same function. Not only "pilgrimes were they alle," but people-whose-clothing-suits-their-profession-and-character-exactly were they alle, and this unites them.

That clothing should so easily raise the issue of profession is reasonable, even inevitable, since of all Chaucer's "relating" categories profession is the most important and interesting, and most profoundly connected with the nature and significance of the poem. By classifying each pilgrim according to his profession, Chaucer raises two sorts of general issues. The largest is the implied generalization, "the profession makes the man." It is worth noting that Chaucer need not have granted so much prominence to professions; possibly he could have avoided profession entirely. He might have given all his pilgrims names, and emphasized interplay among them that arises from traits of character that have nothing to do with their jobs. But the profession dominates each description so much that even when we know, say, that "this worthy lymytour was cleped Huberd," we continue (as Chaucer does) to call him "the Friar." Chaucer has chosen to suppose that distinctions among people arise primarily from their professions, or at least that the most distinctive way of describing them in this public context is through their professions. There is a nice realism here: when strangers meet they regard questions about each other's jobs as acceptable, and Chaucer gives, for the most part, details ascertainable on a superficial acquaintance. But that is a minor feature; the deeper rationale for the emphasis on profession lies in Chaucer's interest in general classes and in his desire to place limits on individuality. Ultimately this emphasis draws them together, obliterates rather than makes distinctions.[2]

We are forced to accept not only the large generalization that the pilgrims' traits of character are professional, but a series of smaller generalizations about each profession as well: that lawyers seem busy, that millers cheat, that pardoners are glib, and so on. Though each pilgrim is endowed with individual life, each is also very much the stereotype or

35

The One and the Many

the ideal representative of his profession or estate: the Squire typifies all squires (and good sons), the Reeve all agents, the Clerk all scholars; the Knight is what all knights, the Parson what all priests, should be. The linguistic staple of the average portrait is professional jargon, words like "lodemenage," "chevyssaunce," "pleyn commissioun," "letuaries." The basis of many portraits is a collection of professional terms; the ultimate in this line is the portrait of the Cook, every detail of which, except the mormal on his shin, is about cooking, and could be applied to any cook. And the emphasis falls very often on the "tricks" of the trade; we learn how many pilgrims manipulate their professional skill to make money.[3]

This professional orientation has been insufficiently acknowledged.[4] Those who emphasize the typical nature of Chaucer's characters usually speak in terms of "human nature," but they speak accurately only to the degree that it is human nature to allow one's profession to shape one's character. Chaucer would have come closer to "human nature" in its ordinary meaning had he given us twenty-nine friars, say, or twenty-nine clerks, all with different traits of personality. The result would have been something at once more far-ranging and more minute, a set of much finer distinctions of character. Instead he chose to operate on the cruder and more generic level of profession. There is a grosser difference between a clerk and a friar than between two clerks or two friars.

The professional emphasis of the General Prologue is reinforced when we pass to the tales and find characters who share professions with certain pilgrims, and find that they share professional characteristics too. Thus there is hardly a detail in the account of the Friar in the General Prologue that is not borne out or extended dramatically in the words and actions of the friar in the Summoner's Tale. He begs well, he is "curteis," he courts the rich, he is ready to grant absolution and easy penance in return for a "good pitaunce," he is charming to women and greets them playfully, he is "lyk a maister." It is possible to interpret this, of course, as a conscious attempt on the part of the Summoner to discredit the pilgrim Friar, but it is far more reasonable to think of Chaucer as working in both cases with a conventional set of comic friar traits.[5] The same can be said of the summoner in the Friar's Tale; the portrait of that summoner which the Friar gives at the beginning simply explains in more detail the extortionary practices touched on in the General Prologue:

> A slyer boy was noon in Engelond;
> For subtilly he hadde his espiaille,
> That taughte hym wher hym myghte availle.
> He koude spare of lecchours oon or two,
> To techen hym to foure and twenty mo. (D1326)
> . . . .
> He hadde eek wenches at his retenue. . . .   (D1355)

This is not substantially different from, only more explicit than,

> In daunger hadde he at his owene gyse
> The yonge girles of the diocise,
> And knew hir conseil, and was al hir reed.   (A665)

One even hears the characteristic voice of the General Prologue here, in the hyperbolic praise of self-interested professional skill ("A slyer boy was noon in Engelond") and in the jargon: not only "espiaille" but the interesting echo in "boy" of "girles" from the General Prologue, both clearly underworld slang. Again, the devil this summoner meets appears to be

> A gay yeman, under a forest syde.
> A bowe he bar, and arwes brighte and kene;
> He hadde upon a courtepy of grene.   (D1382)

This costume deceives the summoner not only because he is stupid, like the pilgrim Summoner, but also because it has indeed the standard yeoman look, as we know from the Knight's Yeoman. And yet another "professional" reprise of the General Prologue in the Friar's Tale is its theme of dishonest agency, which recalls the Reeve at several points. The monk in the Shipman's Tale, like the pilgrim Monk, is "an outridere, that lovede venerie." The merchant in the same tale has business in Flanders, makes a "chevyssaunce," sounds constantly the increase of his winning, and dwells on the importance of keeping his financial status secret; in all these respects he recalls the Merchant of the General Prologue. Symkyn the miller in the Reeve's Tale, though "deynous" in a way that our Miller is not, is like him in piping, wrestling, stealing, and drunkenness. Since the Clerk in the General Prologue is more ideal than type, the various clerks who appear in the tales do not resemble him in essentials. Rather, Nicholas in the Miller's Tale can be seen as the type against which that ideal is placed: he has the "gay sautrie" (A3213) that the pilgrim Clerk rejects; he takes least "cure," not most, of "studie." Yet the fact that we learn of each what lies "at his beddes heed" suggests after all a generic manner of describing a clerk, and Nicholas can play on the clerkly habit of "studie" when it suits his purpose. All six clerks (adding John and Aleyn from the Reeve's Tale, the Wife of Bath's Jankyn, and the clerk of Orleans in the Franklin's Tale) are poor, all operate primarily by their wits and book-learning with mixed results; all but the ideal Clerk are successful in love;[6] Jankyn like Nicholas is "hende" to his Alison (D628).

What this focus on professional stereotypes means for the General Prologue is clear enough: it establishes as an important issue in the poem the relation of the individual (Friar Hubert) to the genus (friar), and of individual subgenera (friar, miller, manciple, etc.) to a still higher genus (profession); and indeed, when that genus is added to other genera such as sex, clothing, wealth, of all those to an even higher genus (human characteristics). The implicit hierarchy carries on the mode of thought introduced by the opening sentence; it forces us to consider the many in relation to the one. This is true, however, of all the categories employed in the portraits. The emphasis on profession has still further implications for the General Prologue and for the whole poem. First of all, it may be noted that the "reprises" of the General Prologue to which I have called attention tend to occur in the fabliaux: the tales of the Miller, Reeve, Shipman, Friar, Summoner. This suggests that the General Prologue may owe its descriptive technique at least in part to that genre. These tales typically commence with descriptions of one or more of the major characters,[7] descriptions which are rich in concrete detail but economical in directing those details toward delineating an apparently special but actually quite typical character; the story works out in some ironic way the consequences of those details of character. Certain "professional" conventions obtain: the clever young cleric will cuckold the bourgeois, trade-proud older husband (Miller's, Reeve's, Shipman's Tales);[8] those who employ their professional skill for dishonest private gain (the summoner, the friar, Symkyn) will eventually be exposed and victimized; there is a special pleasure in unmasking pretension— Absolon's to sex appeal, Symkyn's and his wife's to social position, the friar's to virtue.

The *Canterbury Tales* as a whole follows some of the conventions of this genre; it is a kind of meta-fabliau in which certain tales and pairs of tales, and certain links, are the matter for the acting out of similar professional clashes among the pilgrims described at the beginning. Thus the whole conflict between the Friar and the Summoner, in both the headlinks and their tales, is a "fabliau" introduced by their respective descriptions in the General Prologue. The Friar, because he is more hypocritical about his dishonesty than the Summoner, loses the contest, though the Summoner (like Nicholas) does not escape unscathed. The Miller and the Reeve are opposed in a similar fabliau-like conflict, less conclusive, though probably won by the goliardic Miller. Other fabliau-like professional clashes, not fully developed, but all involving some rebuke or exposure of roguery, occur

between the Host and the Pardoner; the Shipman and the
Merchant; the Host, the Cook, and the Manciple; the Pardoner, the Friar, and the Wife; and between the Clerk and the
Wife (for the poem consistently treats wifehood as a profession, as will become clear). To the degree that the Nuns'
Priest's Tale is an effective satire on women, the Nuns' Priest
is the standard clever cleric of the fabliaux (though he lacks a
description), overcoming Prioress and Wife intellectually as
Nicholas or John and Aleyn or Don John overcome various
women sexually. Since the Monk is dashed (by the Knight—is
the Monk's aping of aristocratic habits in his riding, hunting,
and feasting in part responsible?) and the Pardoner has a go
at the Doctor, the fabliau pattern in which a portrait of a
rogue is followed eventually by some exposure or comeup-
pance holds for all the rogues in the General Prologue except
the Shipman and the lawyer. But then the fabliaux never take
care of everything absolutely neatly.[9]

The basis for all these clashes and exposures is conventional professional animosity, the assumption that certain
professions are inevitably in conflict with others. The Friar
hates the Summoner because summoners snoop into friars'
doings; the Summoner hates the Friar because friars are
beyond summoners' jurisdiction (D1330). The Reeve hates
the Miller because, as an agent for a farm, he must bring
wheat to be ground and is thus vulnerable to being cheated
(this seems a deeper source of his animosity than the business
of carpentry); and the Miller returns his hate, as millers
would, regarding reeves as a major source of their unsavory
reputation. Hosts, manciples, and cooks all deal in victuals,
and can come in conflict with each other in a variety of
ways.[10] That clerks and women stand inevitably in opposition to each other is amply demonstrated by the Wife in her
Prologue. (Common professional interest, on the other hand,
promotes friendship: the lawyer and the Franklin share an
interest in land, the Pardoner and the Summoner in bilking
priests.) The conventional animosity which parsons should
feel toward friars and pardoners has a bearing on the Parson's

Tale (see below, p. 154). Shipmen and merchants are also natural enemies, as their portraits make clear, which may explain why Chaucer apparently reassigned to the Shipman from the Wife a tale in which the butt is a merchant (but he seems to have chosen not to carry out this conflict fully, since the Merchant does not reciprocate). Behind the clash between the Pardoner and the Host may lie the fact that the Pardoner's job causes him to travel. In all this we find Chaucer's willingness to generalize once again at work: he accepts the standard professional animosities.

The professionalism of the fabliau needs further elaboration. I have said that its characters tend to be professional stereotypes, and to be described formally as such; that it makes use of conventional professional animosities; that it exposes professional dishonesty; and I have applied all these features to the poem at large. The exposure of professional dishonesty has a double aspect: it not only involves a final unmasking or embarrassment of the dishonest practitioner; along the way it also exposes or explains in detail, as the General Prologue often does, the "tricks of the trade." Of the fabliaux, the Friar's and Summoner's Tales do this best: each is almost exclusively devoted to a contemptuous account of professional trickery, and each also has a "professional" plot: the characters enact the events of the tales in the course of doing their jobs. In the Shipman's, Miller's, and Reeve's Tales the plot is domestic, not professional, and yet professional characteristics and professional tricks have their place. Thus the domestic shenanigans which the monk and the wife carry on in the Shipman's Tale are wholly based on the character and professional activities of the merchant husband; the students' domestic revenge in the Reeve's Tale is their response to the miller's professional trick; and Nicholas in the Miller's Tale, in carrying out his domestic purpose, capitalizes on the fact that John is away on business, and makes use not only of his own skill as meteorologist but also of John's as carpenter. Furthermore, both the Miller's and Shipman's Tales show us women engaged in the tricky "art" of wifehood: the woman in the latter tale does so most directly, since she sleeps with the monk in order to make money. The Cook's Tale seems intended to focus on the professional characteristics and activities of thieves and whores, perhaps with the satiric intention of implying or suggesting a generalization beyond professions: that all men, whatever their profession, are thieves, all women whores.[11]

Thus the professional interest in the poem seems to take its origin in the fabliaux, and from there to be extended to the General Prologue and the links, and to provide the occasion for a number of the tales: the fabliaux themselves, tales of professional animosity, are told for the purpose of professional animosity, thus becoming themselves elements in the "meta-fabliau" which is the poem, or a significant part of it. Professional interest is extended in another significant way, however, for three of the most profound parts of the poem, the Pardoner's Tale, the Wife of Bath's Prologue, and the Canon's Yeoman's Tale, are also "tricks of the trade" tales.[12] In each we learn the secrets of a profession: of pardoning, of alchemy, and of wifehood.

That the Pardoner and the Canon's Yeoman reveal professional secrets is clear enough (though readers do not ordinarily link them with the fabliaux); that the Wife belongs in this class can be demonstrated readily. Any profession has two ingredients: it must have a body of knowledge or set of skills, which are initially learned through a combination of teaching and on-the-job training, which can be taught to others, and in the exercise of which some practitioners become more expert than others; and it must engender a product or provide a service, both so that it fulfils some social function and so that one can make money by it. In the professional fabliau, there is the further requirement that the practitioner must use his skill to deceive or exploit others, for selfish ends; the real service is to the self. The Wife's wifehood amply fills these requirements.[13] In fulfilling the social function of wife, in "paying her debt," she has made money by marrying rich old men and forcing them to sign their property over to her; it is essential that they be old as well as rich, so that they will die soon and enable her both to come fully into the property and to go out fortune hunting again. Nor is money incidental: for the Wife as for the Pardoner money is primary; his "myn entente is nat but for to wynne" (C403) is matched by her

> Wynne whoso may, for al is for to selle;
> With empty hand men may none haukes lure.
> For wynnyng wolde I al his lust endure.   (D416)

The skills required, and her mastery of them, are no less evident. She learned them first by a kind of apprenticeship to her mother ("I folwed ay my dames loore"[14] [D583]), and has perfected them in the five separate positions she has held since emerging from her apprenticeship:

> Diverse scoles maken parfyt clerkes,
> And diverse practyk in many sondry werkes
> Maketh the werkman parfyt sekirly;
> Of fyve husbondes scoleiyng am I.
> Welcome the sixte, whan that evere he shal.   (D45)

These are rich lines indeed. She distinguishes between schooling, the way the clerk learns, and "practyk," the way the workman learns. Since she left her mother's knee to enter into actual marriage, in whose "actes" she spends "the flour of al [her] age" (D114), she is surely a practitioner, a workman, using her "instrument," not a mere student; furthermore, she everywhere disdains the whole world of clerks; and yet she claims here to be, not "practicing," but "scoleiyng." Wifehood, she implies, is a profession whose skills are so refined and so deep that one goes on learning through a lifetime of practice. Yet despite her learner's stance ("welcome the sixte"), she has achieved "maistrie," she is a master wife, an "archwife," as the Clerk calls her, "expert in al [her] age" (D 174). Though by "maistrie" she means mainly supremacy over her husband, she includes in it the notion of placing him in the role of apprentice (be he old or young, foolish or learned), and is surely conscious that she has achieved the formal status of "mastery" in her profession. Of course "master" means "teacher"; like other master craftsmen (and like clerks who are Masters of Arts), she is qualified to "teche us yonge men of youre praktike," as the Pardoner asks her, and to train as well the "wise wyves, that kan understonde" whom she lectures on how to lecture their husbands (D 224-381); she also seems to be a qualified *magister artium* in her clerkly ability to conduct a formal disputation on the theology of marriage: she was "schooled" by Jankyn in a way she did not expect.[15]

Of course all readers recognize the irony of her learning, that despite her exaltation of experience over authority she has not only learned from authority (from her mother, from Jankyn and his book, and from the "school" of marriage, a metaphor of her own making in which she seems to acknowledge that experience is authority), she has become an authority, and speaks authoritatively. These ironies can also be expressed in professional terms, however, and so in a way that relates them more clearly to the rest of the poem. Though as a woman she may seem not to have a profession at all, and to stand at the opposite pole from clerks, those quintessentially skilled males, she makes it clear in fact that she is a "real pro," a Master of Arts in marriage, and even a better professional than the average clerk since she is not only skilled but rich. The irony is all the more effective because on the surface she holds to the fiction that she is not a professional at all. Nor is the irony turned entirely toward her: the vanity implicit in male professionalism is dealt a deadly blow. And the generalizing thrust that the emphasis on professionalism always entails is very much present here: if even clerks and women are one, where is the many?

A further connection, also ultimately related to professionalism, which the Wife of Bath's Prologue, the Pardoner's Tale, and the Canon's Yeoman's Tale have with the fabliaux is

44

that each moves toward a vivid climactic scene in which the skill of the practitioner finds its inevitable denouement. Three examples from the fabliaux are the bed scene in the Shipman's Tale, in which the wife finds the words to satisfy her husband; the "Water!" scene in the Miller's Tale, in which Nicholas gets burnt for enacting his skill too zealously; and the fart scene in the Summoner's Tale, which forces the friar to see how empty his rhetorical skill really is. The Canon and the Pardoner both find their skill thwarted: the former when his pot explodes, the latter when his attempt to sell the Host pardon meets with gross rebuff. The Wife, however, handles her climax, the book scene with Jankyn, with a transcendent skill that has interesting implications for the whole issue of professionalism and its relation to generality.

In professional terms, the marriage to Jankyn is a mistake, a wrong turn in her career. Since he is poor, and only twenty, and since she signs her property over to him, she can make no money off him. She is, furthermore, now the customer rather than the merchant; it is he who is "daungerous" in "outing" his "chaffare." There is therefore insufficient "practyk"; instead there is formal schooling in anti-feminist literature, of which he is master. Where once she lectured her old husbands on the things she claimed they accused her of, things of which she was in fact guilty though they had not so accused her, now she is lectured by her husband on things of which she is not guilty. Her professional status lies in doubt. This state of affairs is the rough equivalent of the unmasking or embarrassment of the deceptive practitioner in the fabliaux. But it does not last.

For she reverses everything dramatically when she tears the page (or pages)[16] from the book and knocks Jankyn backward into the fire. Since, as it turns out, this was just the right thing to do, it constitutes a mastering, by her practical knowledge, of his book-learning. When he gets up and hits her back, she is still the winner, both because she has (artfully) finally drawn a natural reaction from him, and because she conquers him further from her prone position: like Grisilde, but more rapidly, in her very passiveness she forces her husband to recognize his cruelty and repent of it. Even the deafness he has caused has its value: she cannot now hear his lectures so well. The eventual result is a firm re-establishment of both her mastery and her wealth.

From another point of view, however, she can be seen to have evaded the fabliau conventions, and the stereotyping they imply. This is evident not only because she actually marries the parish clerk (as if Alison in the Miller's Tale had married Absolon), but especially because she is the older party. In her first three marriages the standard fabliau January-May situation obtained; she has gone beyond the fabliau simply by living on—and carrying on her story—to reach a level of unconventionality with which the fabliau is not prepared to deal. Nor can the fabliau sustain any genuine extension of time: its events must take place swiftly, lest the characters develop. Fabliaux are similarly static in that in them professional skills are given, not developed: we do not see Nicholas learning more about meteorology, or the friar about rhetoric, or the summoner about extortion; what they learn is not new skills but the limits of the skills they have. The Wife keeps learning, and keeps getting older, and so transcends the fabliau, and transcends generalization: she is never more individual than in her "unprofessional" marriage to Jankyn. Nor does her individuality suffer much when she regains her mastery; not only does she exercise it with a new and quite unprofessional mellowness, she retains the individuating mark of her deafness. It does not go away, like Nicholas's scalding.

The Pardoner's professionalism, in contrast, for all his startling distinctiveness, remains wholly within the fabliau convention of professional trickery. He is so thoroughgoing a professional that, though he seems, like the Wife, only to be describing his art, or at most to be giving a merely instructive or entertaining example of it, he is actually plying it, as his appeal for funds at the end indicates. For the best way to understand him is to take him absolutely literally when he says "myn entente is nat but for to wynne." He intends from the start to "take" the pilgrims, to make money from them; but since they are not his usual ignorant audience, he decides, confident and skillful rhetorician that he is, to render them benevolent by seeming to confide in them, as Nicholas seems to confide in John the carpenter.[17] Surely he realizes the risk he takes; his performance can be thought of as like Nicholas's or the friar's or the summoner's, an experiment in virtuosity, in the limits of his ability. The Pardoner, perhaps like the Friar's summoner, is *all* professional. He has no simply human element left, so that he expects not to mind—or does not even consider—the emotional pain he will suffer if he fails. Even if we conceive of his final appeal as only playacting, a sophisticated entertainment, we still must see him as unable to escape his professional character, since it depends entirely for its effect on his rhetorical skill.[18] As I have said, there is a further professional element in his insulting appeal to the Host, since traveling men and innkeepers have the kind of customer-purveyor relationship that breeds professional animosity, and more especially since the Pardoner makes money by vilifying taverns in his sermons. The Host's reply is anti-rhetorical, calling a spade a spade, and it finds a limit to the Pardoner's skill since it renders him speechless. The final blow to his professional character comes when the Knight makes him kiss the Host: he must use his mouth silently in a genuine act of pardon, not a professional "act" of false pardon. The Pardoner by profession becomes a pardoner in private. This is a "professional" irony; though both are profound poems, the Pardoner's Tale, unlike the Wife of Bath's Prologue, achieves its profundity without transcending the conventions of professional exploitation. The Pardoner attains his distinction in the brilliance of his skill, and in the breathtaking gulf between the mystical ideal of pardon and the utterly venal uses to which he puts it; but he is de-individualized, brought into unity with the rest of mankind, because in the very act of establishing his distinctiveness he fits himself also to the very general sterotype of the skilled, manipulative, exposed professional.

Another one-and-many aspect of the professional tales is the issue of privacy ("pryvetee") versus exposure. The professional deceiver requires privacy, obviously, or the deceit will go awry. But his need for privacy suggests also that he is under the delusion that what he is doing is unique; his maintenance of privacy is an assertion of individuality, since it erects a barrier between him and others. He enjoys a sense of uniqueness because he knows that his view of himself differs from the way others see him. Exposure destroys this uniqueness: it effaces the barrier, and the separate views, and it enables the public who learn the truth to classify the exposed practitioner as a fraud. The poem is general in that it engages in exposure: it makes us see each apparently unique professional as not only sharing the conventional traits of his profession but as belonging to the still more general class of fraudulent practitioner, a category that, the poem persuades us, embraces all professions.

I have been speaking here, of course, as if the fraudulent practitioner were wholly bent on achieving and maintaining privacy and protecting his individuality. But that is not exactly true: the recognition of unifying elements in the poem is so strong that even these arch-individualists share in it. In the first place, there is nothing in the poem to suggest, despite the ironies I have been describing, that the various practitioners do not themselves recognize what they have in common. The Summoner's friar, for example, is presumably aware that other friars are like him, as Nicholas must know that other clever young students act as he does. That is why the victim of a fraud must be someone wholly different from the practitioner: pardoners victimize parsons and congregations, not other pardoners, and so on. The Wife, though she may not be wholly aware of her likeness to fraudulent practitioners in general, is obviously aware of her likeness to other women. Indeed it may be said that each professional deceiver in the poem is fully conscious of his links with his own craft, though he may regard himself as a superior specimen; it is only the higher generalization—his links with

48

"professionals" in general—that eludes him. And other associations qualify his privacy: Nicholas, like anyone whose goal
is not money but sex, must share his plans with Alison; the
Summoner's friar is at least partially in league, in brotherhood, with the other beggars in his house, and the Friar's
summoner with his "espiaille" (and, so he thinks, with the
fiend he meets).

These partial or tentative recognitions of fellowship, since
they reveal that even the arch-individualist acknowledges his
need for others, may be seen to lie behind the numerous
confessions that these "privee" operators make. On the surface, of course, confession is a mistake, a weakness, a chance
of exposure one must not take. Thus the Friar's summoner's
troubles begin when he enters into partnership with the devil.
Though he never directly admits that he is a summoner, he
admits that he extorts, and it is his exhibitionist urge to ply his
trade in the presence of this "partner" that damns him. A
fundamental point of the tale is that the summoner compromises his effectiveness by violating the secrecy and privacy
that must characterize all he does. We are not told why he
does it: of course the Friar means to imply that summoners
are drawn instinctively into alliance with devils, and that they
are just plain stupid; but he seems to imply too a kind of
compulsive boastfulness, an ineluctable urge in the fraudulent practitioner to put his skill on display, born apparently of
the very pressure to be secret that ordinarily obtains.[19]

A similar compulsion plays a role in other fabliaux, though
less disastrously. In the Miller's Tale, Nicholas shows it when
he puts his buttocks out the window to Absolon: "And out his
ers he putteth pryvely" (A3802). Though he hardly regards
this as a revelation (trusting that in this area the difference
between male and female is indistinguishable, at least to
Absolon's lips in the dark), and though he does it "pryvely,"
the fact is that for the first time in this tale of an "inside job"
Nicholas is "out," and the result is that his secret doings are in
far greater danger of being revealed than he intended
(though he and Alison find the words to quell the danger). In

the Reeve's Tale, Aleyn's urge to tell John of his success with the miller's daughter precipitates mayhem (although here too the danger is only momentary, and the error works ultimately in Aleyn's and John's favor, since one can imagine various more perilous outcomes had Aleyn simply fallen asleep in the miller's bed; furthermore, in view of the miller's ambitions for his daughter, the clerks' revenge on him relies for its fulness on his knowing she has lost her virginity).

The Summoner's Tale is a complex exploration of the interplay between "pryvetee" and confession. It begins publicly, with the friar preaching in church, moves to the domestic scene of Thomas's house, where, the friar's "felawe" and Thomas's wife having been separately dismissed, Thomas's "confession" takes place in utter privacy; then moves back to the public scene of the lord's court, before which the friar makes *his* confession. Of course, Thomas never confesses; the friar's attempts "to grope tendrely a conscience" (D1817) net him nothing, as his attempt on Thomas's property, which culminates in physical groping for "a thyng that I have hyd in pryvetee" (D2143) nets him only a fart. The real confession takes place before the lord and lady and their retinue. The friar is unaware of its manifold ironies: that he is supposed to be their confessor; that he is at first utterly speechless, then responds to the lord's and lady's gropings, their confessor's patter ("tel me al" [D 2189], "Is ther aught elles? telle me feithfully" [D2203]); that his whole confession is the product of wrath, the very sin on which he preached so eloquently to Thomas; that the fart characterizes him precisely. This confession is utterly compulsive and irrational. Though he is seeking retribution, it merely compounds his shame; and it differs from the confessions in the other fabliaux in that it is a confession of failure. It leaves the friar utterly without "pryvetee," without self-respect; now both the world at large and he himself know that at bottom he is only air, sound, and smell—no substance.

These variously compelled and variously harmful confessions form the background, and something of a rationale, for the confessions of the Pardoner, the Wife, and the Canon's Yeoman. Each in its own way is motivated by a desire to recognize or achieve fellowship. The Pardoner's has the smallest dose of such desire, since, as I have argued, it is best interpreted not as an attempt to achieve fellowship with the other pilgrims but to con them out of their money in an unusual way. Even so, the Pardoner's choice of the daring and unsuccessful device of apparent confession is explainable in terms of the compulsion of the practitioner to reveal and exhibit. He is surprisingly similar to the Frair's summoner, who hopes to profit by his very self-revelation: that summoner's apparently generous offer to go halves on all profits with the devil is based on his assumption that even more loot is likely to come in the devil's way than in his own. The Canon's Yeoman's confession is the opposite of the Pardoner's. It stems, apparently, from the compulsive need for fellowship—he cannot resist answering the Host's prodding questions—but it succeeds where the Pardoner's does not because it replaces rather than serves the desire to "win," and because on his part it is a confession more of gullibility than of gulling, the burden of manipulation being placed almost wholly on the Canon. Nevertheless, the Yeoman does not always avoid a certain boastful tone: beneath his derisiveness lurks a substantial residue of pride in his professional knowledge of terms and processes. The germ of the Wife's confession can be seen in the performances of Nicholas and Aleyn: it arises from the exuberance of winning at sex, or from the exhibitionism that sex often involves; and like Nicholas and Aleyn she is not hurt by it. Indeed, just as Nicholas's unwary appearance at the window leads finally to an integrated scene, in which the whole community laughs together at the carpenter, so the Wife's urge to reveal leads, because of her tremendous synthetic power, to integration: of herself with the company of pilgrims; of herself with all womanhood; of herself with herself, as she discovers and imposes, through the process of creative memory, apparently for the first time, a unified vision on her life.

51

Let me summarize the argument of this chapter. The emphasis on professions in the General Prologue limits the individuality of the pilgrims not only by identifying them professionally and associating them with professional stereotypes, but by implying that it is possible to generalize about professionalism itself. This emphasis, and the generalizing force it embodies, continues into the main body of the poem: into the links, in which various conventional professional animosities develop; into the fabliaux, which like the poem itself typically begin with "professional" character descriptions and carry out their implication in a plot which relies on professional activity or develops a conflict between members of different professions; and in the discourses of the Wife, the Pardoner, and the Canon's Yeoman, each of which, like many fabliaux and many of the portraits in the General Prologue, is an account of fraudulent professional practice. A particular major issue which professional fraud raises is that of the conflict between privacy and confession.

All this extends the poem's thrust toward unity. More than a third of the poem (the General Prologue, the links, the six "professional" fabliaux and the three major tales of Pardoner, Wife, and Canon's Yeoman) has a very strong professional emphasis. To these one might add the Nuns' Priest's Tale, which satirizes professionalism by examining the "practyk" of roosters, foxes, and hens; the Merchant's Tale and the Manciple's Tale, in which wives enact their conventional professional skills; and in minor ways *Melibee*, *Sir Thopas*, and even the Parson's Tale.[20] A simple result of this extension of certain conventions of the fabliau into so much of the poem is that it moves us closer to a sense of unity of genre, farther from a sense of unchecked variety; the fabliau constitutes a governing mode. And the generality of professions, and of professionalism itself, provides a constant limitation on individuality: the uniqueness of even such richly presented characters as the Wife and the Pardoner is set against the numerous traits they share with other members of their professions and with professionals in general. Finally, the interplay between privacy and confession is a particular arena for displaying the relationship between one and many; but the thrust here is also in the direction of unity, not only because all the fraudulent practitioners seek privacy, but also because this privacy is regularly replaced by public exposure and a movement toward integration.

3. Men and Women and Marriage

In the previous chapter I tried to show that beneath the superficial variety of persons Chaucer conceived of adult human character as professional. Here I wish to show that, in parallel with this, he conceived of human character as simply divisible into male and female. Women have one set of characteristics, men another; sex is of overriding importance—if you know a person's sex you know virtually everything about him.[1] Furthermore, the twain do not meet: though all men are like each other, and all women are like each other, men are emphatically not like women. If Chaucer cannot be said to treat people as individuals, neither can he be said to treat "human nature," but only "male nature" and "female nature" (always excepting the ironic suggestion that womanhood is a profession). He reaches this level of division or generalization and stops. He probes beneath the many and finds, not the one, but the two.

This theme takes its beginning in the juxtaposition of the Wife and the Parson in the General Prologue (A445-528). (It is the Wife's regular fate to be coupled with a clerk.) Both are introduced by their sex rather than by their profession (again putting aside momentarily the notion that wifehood is a profession): "a good Wif was ther of biside Bathe," "a good man was ther of religioun." These echoing lines are an invitation to see the portraits as complementary. The varying words after "was ther of" give a clue at once to Chaucer's characteristic way of differentiating between women and men: "biside Bathe" is a real, particular place; "religioun" substitutes an abstraction for a locality. This contrast continues: the Wife is solidly physical, earthbound, limited and particularized by her clothing, her bodily characteristics, her personal history and geography; the Parson is connected with no time, and with no particular place but "a toun"; we learn nothing of what he looks like or where he has been. He is spiritual, idealized and idealistic, abstractly described and committed to abstractions. "He koude in litel thyng have suffisaunce," and the portrait likewise has little to do with things. The Wife has many things, and they tend to be big, not little: ten-pound kerchiefs, a broad hat, large hips; even a non-thing, the space between her teeth, is big. She is associated with multiplicity: five husbands (and "oother compaignye"), three trips to Jerusalem, "many a straunge strem," many remedies of love. He is single and single-minded, and learned rather than knowing; his learning seems confined to a single book, "Cristes gospel." She is expansive, he is inward and intense. The Wife is fixed in time, by phrases like "al hir lyve" and "in youthe," by pluperfect verbs ("hadde she been"), even by her five husbands, whom she can only have had in succession; but in the portrait of the Parson time is suspended in a kind of continuous present (in the narrative, an imperfect).

The rhetorical patterns of the two portraits reinforce these contrasts. The Parson is consistently defined by a kind of *via contraria:* his single-mindedness is accentuated by a series of contrasts and denials. His word is "but": "And was a povre Persoun of a toun, / But riche he was of holy thoght and werk"; "Ful looth were hym to cursen . . . / But rather wolde he yeven"; "Wyd was his parisshe . . . / But he lefte nat . . . / . . . to visite / The ferreste"; "He sette nat his benefice to hyre / . . . But dwelte at hoom"; "He was a shepherde and noght a mercenarie"; "He was to synful men nat despitous / . . . But in his techyng discreet and benygne." Finally,

He waited after no pompe and reverence,
Ne maked him a spiced conscience,
But Cristes loore and his apostles twelve
He taughte, but first he folwed it hymselve.   (A528)

This climactic sentence finishes off the process of refinement
by two negatives and a double "but." The whole effect is of
precise definition, strengthening our sense of the Parson's
unified devotion to his ideal by a process of rejection of other
possibilities.

This rhetorical pattern is altogether absent in the description of the Wife. Her word is "and," not "but." The description is wholly paratactic. It adds factual details in a random
and realistic way, suggesting that the Wife is the sum of her
multiple accidental characteristics and experiences, defined
without reference to any unifying ideal. I do not mean that
she is inconsistent or characterless—indeed the rich line "she
koude muche of wandrynge by the weye" brings together
many things, including her special interest in footwear—my
point is that the relaxed and "experiential" rhetorical style of
the portrait suits her approach to life, which also wanders by
the way, and is as opposed to the style of the Parson's portrait
as she is to him. Indeed, a final implicit contrastive statement
about the Parson is "he was not like the Wife, but . . . " One
fact of vital importance in the juxtaposition of the two
portraits is that the Wife's is first.[2]

These two portraits also suggest, in their respective "professional" dimensions, a constant interrelationship between
the emphases in the poem on professionalism and on generic
sexual differences. Men and women are divided sharply by
their relation to professionalism. The distinction can be
stated in either of two ways: either "all men have professions,
few women do," or "men have many different professions,
women essentially only one." As I have tried to demonstrate
in the previous chapter, it is the first formulation that is true at
the surface or apparent level of the poem; the second is never
stated, but is constantly present at a "deeper" ironic level. If

we consider the surface level first, we see the distinction operating clearly in our two model portraits. Everything said about the Parson relates to his profession. This may seem to detract from his role as representative male, since not all males are parsons, but actually strengthens it, since all males have professions and are primarily characterized by them. In contrast, nothing said about the Wife, unless we count the numerous references to the clothing she wears, relates to her profession of clothmaking. Whereas his character derives from his profession, hers derives from her sex. One feels, indeed, that her clothmaking, like Penelope's weaving in the *Odyssey,* confirms her womanhood, since "spynnyng God hath yive / To wommen kyndely" (D402).[3] Alternatively, one can say that, at the "deeper" level, the Wife's portrait *is* professional: all the details relate to her profession of wifehood. Either way she represents the relation of women to professionalism that is standard in the poem.

This professional distinction between the sexes, particularly if formulated in the "deeper" way—"men have many different professions, women essentially only one"—has a number of clear effects on the nature of the poem. It accounts, first of all, for the disproportionate sexual composition of the pilgrimage, twenty-six men (counting the Host and the Canon's Yeoman but only one Nuns' Priest) to three women; and for a further, if less extreme, disproportion of males to females among the major characters in the tales.[4] This disproportion is mirrored in the Wife's having had five husbands, as well as in the hordes of male clerks who populate her imagination; it is parodied by being reversed in the cases of the Nuns' Priest and Chauntecleer. The world of the *Canterbury Tales* is a man's world—except, of course, in that there lurks everywhere the suggestion, which can be interpreted either cynically or honorably, that one woman is the equal of a heap of men.

A second effect of the apparent variety among males and unity among females that professionalism engenders is that the poem is filled with general statements about women, whereas very few are made of men.

Men and Women and Marriage

Aside from the scene in the Merchant's Tale between Pluto and Proserpine, to be examined in detail shortly, I find only four unequivocal generalizations about men. Arcite says, "a man moot nedes love, maugree his heed" (A1169). The Man of Law, exclaiming against Donegild's plot to slander Custance, cries "fy, mannysh, fy!" (B782), implying, that is, that such cruel plots are the property of men. The Clerk says of Walter at his marriage, "the peple hym helde / A prudent man, and that is seyn ful selde" (E427). (Here "that" probably refers to the whole preceding clause, not just to "a prudent man," but it amounts to the same thing: to say "people seldom consider a man prudent" is to regard "men are not prudent" as a commonly accepted generalization. The Clerk actually makes several further generalizations to the same effect: that the desire of a husband to test his wife "bifalleth tymes mo" [E449]; that "wedded men ne knowe no mesure / Whan that they fynde a pacient creature" [E623]; and—though said of "folk," clearly meant of men—

> ther been folk of swich condicion
> That whan they have a certein purpos take,
> They kan nat stynte of hire entencion,
> But, right as they were bounden to a stake,
> They wol nat of that firste purpos slake.   [E705])

And finally, Justinus in the Merchant's Tale, listing the properties of a prospective wife, says one must make sure she is not "mannyssh wood," i.e., not given to imprudent, crazy schemes or idées fixes such as Walter's, Arcite's, or the mannish Donegild's. It is interesting that all four of these places (counting the Clerk's as one) touch on the male penchant to be overcome by an idea. To these unequivocal cases one might add the nine occurrences of the adjective "manly," implying such conventional male characteristics as capable, courageous, physically imposing, commanding, and—in the Parson's Tale, with etymological awareness—virtuous. All the other generalizations about men occur in the con-

59

text of generalizations about women, or in comparisons of men to women.[5] The Franklin says, "Wommen, of kynde, desiren libertee," then adds, "and so doon men" (F770). The Wife says that men cannot lie "half so boldely" as women (D227), and are more reasonable than women (D442). Melibee quotes Solomon: "of a thousand men . . . I foond o good man, but certes, of alle wommen, good womman foond I nevere" (B2247). The Clerk says that men are praised for humility and truth, but that women have a greater capacity for both (E932-38). January says that a wedded man leads a blissful life; but this is merely a vehicle for the Merchant's implication that wives make their husbands unhappy. Similarly, May's accusation that "men been evere untrewe," and accuse women of infidelity to cover up their own (E2203ff.), is a harsh piece of irony by the Merchant, since the next thing May does is signal to Damian to climb the tree. May is merely doing what the Wife advises wise women to do: take the initiative boldly, accuse your husband of accusing you. Finally, the Manciple speaks at length (H155-86) to the effect that "appetit flemeth discrecioun," that is, low nature resists dicipline, then claims,

> Alle thise ensamples [bird, cat, she-wolf] speke I by thise
> men
> That been untrewe, and no thyng by wommen.
> For men han evere a likerous appetit
> On lower thyng to parformen hire delit
> Than on hire wyves.   (H191)

But this is surely tongue-in-cheek, not only in view of the sex of the she-wolf, but because the Manciple then applies it all to Phebus's wife, who deceives him for someone "under hym," "a man of litel reputacioun" (H199). Thus of the generalizations about men, rare to begin with, a number are merely the by-product of, or a vehicle for, generalizations about women.

These latter abound. The central document is, of course,

the Wife of Bath's Tale, with its unequivocal and universally accepted statement that "wommen desiren to have sovereynetee" (D1038), a statement that does not contradict the wealth of subordinate statements offered along the way, both in the tale and in the prologue, about women's desires and habits. Nor does it contradict what is said of women's various desires by the wife in the Shipman's Tale (B1363-67) and Pertelote in the Nuns' Priest's Tale (B4102-07). Indeed the issue of "what women most desire" is a good small instance of the one and the many; the knight in the Wife's Tale is offered many opinions on what women most desire—no two creatures agree—but eventually finds a formulation which is universally accepted and which subsumes all the others; and the issue calls forth statements about both men and women at once, so that it is a teasing question whether to place this issue under "men" or under "women."

A rough count reveals upwards of 140 general statements about women in the poem. After the Wife's Prologue and Tale, *Melibee* and the Merchant's Tale, wherein the extreme issue is debated whether there is such a thing as a good woman at all, are especially full of these generalizations. The assumption, implication, or statement that all women are bad, particularly in its specific form that all wives are untrue, is made not only by Melibee and Pluto but by the Miller, the Pardoner (who assumes that all the wives in the congregation will want a cure for jealousy in their husbands), and the Manciple. The similarly extreme statement that *mulier est hominis confusio* (which applies literally to Eve, since *confusio* means "ruin," i. e., "damnation"), both made and unmade by Chauntecleer, is made by Jankyn ("womman was the los of al mankynde" [D720]), by the Monk ("for wommen shal hym bryngen to meschaunce" [B3252]), and by both the Man of Law ("Thou [Satan] madest Eva brynge us in servage" [B368]) and Custance ("thurgh wommans eggement / Mankynde was lorn" [B843]), put in her old husbands' mouths by the Wife of Bath ("Thou seyest, right as wormes shende a tree, / Right so a wyf destroyeth hire housbonde"

[D377]), referred to by Pluto ("the treson whiche that womman dooth to man" [E2239]), and opposed by Prudence ("if
that wommen were nat goode . . . oure Lord God of hevene
wolde neither han wroght hem, ne called hem help of man,
but rather confusioun of man" [B2296]—evidently the source
of Chauntecleer's double-edged locution), by the Parson
("God made womman of the ryb of Adam, for womman
sholde be felawe unto man" [I928]), and by the ironic Merchant ("He which that hath no wyf, I holde hym shent"
[E1320]; "wyf is mannes helpe and his confort" [E1331]).
Less extreme examples come from almost everywhere in
the poem. The Knight: "For wommen, as to speken in com-
une, / They folwen al the favour of Fortune" (A2682).[6] The
Prioress refers to "modres pitee"; the Knight, and the contrite
attackers at the end of *Melibee*, to "wommanly pitee" (B593,
A3083, B2940). The Summoner's friar: "Ther nys, ywis, no
serpent so cruel, / Whan man tret on his tayl, ne half so fel, /
As womman is, whan she hath caught an ire" (D2003); the
Squire: "thise olde wommen that been gladly wyse" (F376);
the Franklin: "wepeth she and siketh, / As doon thise noble
wyves whan hem liketh" (F818); the Physician: "For al to
soone may she lerne loore / Of boldnesse whan she woxen is a
wyf" (C71). The Canon's Yeoman considers that "carolynge"
and "to speke of love and wommanhede" are as natural to
women as singing in birds and hardy deeds in knights (G1346)
(note the equal generic status given here to all women, all
birds, and a single male profession). Though the Parson in
general goes beyond sex, being the only speaker who regularly generalizes about "men and wommen," we learn from
him such general facts as "ther as the womman hath the
maistrie, she maketh to muche desray" (I927), and that
woman "kan nat paciently suffre" (I928).
   The only tales that make no generalizations of any sort
about women are the Reeve's and the Cook's (though these
strongly imply that women are untrue),[7] *Thopas*, the Friar's,
and the Second Nun's (though this strongly implies that
women are good). The Clerk, the Man of Law, and the Squire

Men and Women and Marriage

are all anxious, against the tide, to generalize favorably about
women. Their generalizations range from the Squire's mild
reference to "wommanly benignytee" (F486) or his statement
that Canacee is "ful mesurable, as wommen be" (F362);
through the Man of Law's praise of Chaucer for commending
"wifhod" (B76), his calling the Sultan's mother a "feyned
womman" for being a "nest of every vice" (B362, 364),[8] and
his sympathetic admission that "wommen are born to
thraldom and penance" (B286); to the Clerk's vigorous claim:

> Men speke of Job, and moost for his humblesse,
> As clerkes, whan hem list, kan wel endite,
> Namely of men, but as in soothfastnesse,
> Though clerkes preise wommen but a lite,
> Ther kan no man in humblesse hym acquite
> As wommen kan, ne kan been half so trewe
> As wommen been, but it be falle of newe.   (E938)

(If the Clerk seems here to claim that in praising Grisilde, and
women in general, he escapes the professional stereotype of
clerks, we should recall the Wife's qualification: "it is an
impossible / That any clerk wol speke good of wyves, / But if
it be of holy seintes lyves" [D690]. That Grisilde is a "holy
seint" is abundantly clear from the Clerk's ending: she is a
symbol of the relation of the soul to God; it would be hard
today to find "in al a toun Grisildis thre or two"; it is "a storie
of . . . mervaille" [E1145ff; 1165; 1186]. He fits both parts of the
Wife's account of how clerks speak of women: through most
of his tale he praises a "holy seint"; at the end, and in his
envoy, as if the pressure of sustaining that rarer side of
clerkliness is too much for him, he adopts the standard
sardonic clerkly stance. He does so, of course, "with lusty
herte, fressh and grene" [E1173], but so does Jankyn.)

The fact that many of these generalizations about women
contradict each other hardly matters; they are merely one
more instance in the poem of diversity of opinion. What
seems more important is the underlying unity that the habit of

63

generalization implies: virtually everyone in the poem assumes that women are susceptible of generalization. Against this oneness Chaucer sets the fact that the generalizations vary. But they do not vary much. As opposed to the apparent variety in men, women are seen as either very, very good or very, very bad. The Wife's generalization about clerks, that they speak ill of all women except saints, is borne out in this clerkish book. Just as the poem resists generalizations about human nature, stopping short of unity at the twoness of the sexes, so the generalizations about women stop short at the twoness of "wikked wyves" and "holy seintes." This twoness is represented in the General Prologue by the inclusion of the Prioress and the Wife—no more and no less.[9] But the Prioress is no saint, of course, and as against the apparent irreducibility of the division into two types that these "authoritative" generalizations imply, the "experience" of the poem drives us toward a less divided view, inviting us to see even such saints as Custance and Grisilde as sharing certain basic female traits, as I shall suggest.

The "professional" distinction between men and women has, in sum, two large effects on the poem: it accounts for the greater number and apparent variety of male characters, and it accounts for the huge discrepancy between the number of generalizations about women and about men. The need for professional expertise also accounts for a general emphasis on male learning, a subject I shall take up shortly. Of course it must be emphasized that despite these clear effects professional male variety is only superficial; the ironic perception that a general "professionalism" underlies it, and is indeed shared by women, undercuts male pretensions to individuality and pride in learning. Whereas the notion that "women are all alike" is open, constantly explicitly entertained, the notion that "men are all alike," and the further notion that "everyone is a professional," are hidden, and yet clearly discernible.

The generic contrast between men and women, initiated in the General Prologue in the coupling of the Wife and Parson,

Men and Women and Marriage

is at issue throughout the tales: Chaucer's women are in
general earthbound and solid, his men searchers after abstract ideals (often foolish).[10] We see this most clearly in a set
of couples who repeat the same basic contrast as that between the Parson and the Wife: Nicholas (also John, also
Absolon) and Alison, Chauntecleer and Pertelote, Walter and
Grisilde, Melibee and Prudence, January and May, Pluto and
Proserpine, Alice and Jankyn, Herry Bailly and Goodelief.
All of these males are given in various ways to ideas and to
"high" things. Nicholas lives upstairs where he studies the
skies and works his clerkish subtleties on John and others;
though eventually he leaves John up in the beams while he
descends to Alison's bed, his weakness for scheming eventually causes him to get up and stay up. Alison has a more
natural and successful sense of how to use her body. John's
superstition and absorption in his work, and Absolon's devotion to an ideal of courtly love, extend the contrast to Alison's
naturalness.

Chauntecleer is better schooled than Pertelote, wants to
stay up in the beams, argues grandly that his dreams come
from God, lifts his head high (and closes his eyes) when he
sings. He is perhaps the fullest comic version Chaucer gives
of male peculiarities: cocky in all senses, an "idealist" and not
a "realist," foolhardy not brave, proud of his professional
skill, boastful yet fondly overcome by female charm. Pertelote's sturdy insistence that Chauntecleer's dream is due to
indigestion, that is, has a "low" and physical source, is equally
the quintessence of Chaucerian femaleness, which has its
comic exposure in her character as a dumb cluck and in her
refusal to grant any credit at all to his lofty notions, which turn
out to be accurate. Men have public responsibilities that
require imagination, intelligence, and verve, and inevitably
lead them to overestimate their importance; women warm
the nest, care more for their husbands' health than for their
business affairs or their deep fears and hopes, peck away at
their vanity, and chatter emptily. Men are farsighted (and
near blind), women nearsighted (and not so easily tripped

up). A man gets in trouble when he reveals his secrets to his wife. A man at home is often outnumbered by women, but the outside professional world is a man's world, a fox-eat-rooster world. In this professional world, fox and rooster ply their separate professional skills: the rooster crows, the fox preys on roosters. Their professional differences suggest that men are divisible into more separate types than women, and yet they share many male traits. Both are clever, but think themselves cleverer than they are; both are articulate speakers, but speak themselves into trouble. If Chauntecleer experiences a final sudden access of common sense, it comes about only because the fox's male vanity is even greater than his. He ends up "heighe upon a tree" (B4607).[11]

Melibee and Prudence, and Walter and Grisilde, present slightly different versions of what is essentially the same contrast. Melibee and Walter are "outrageous" rather than intelligent; both have a fixed idea to which they hold resolutely in defiance of common sense, and which arises from their inflated self-importance, a misplaced devotion to an ideal of political authority. Though Prudence is the wordier, she and Grisilde have much in common both with each other and with the female stereotype. Grisilde is praised for her prudence (E1022) and Prudence for her patience (B2254), and patience is a regular refrain in Prudence's advice to Melibee. Both eventually win their husbands into compliance through their flexible and solid ("sad") common sense. Prudence, to be sure, seems more male than female in her knowledge of the authorities, but her essential femininity and her right to be associated with other women in the poem emerge in her winning the maistrie through a combination of patience and energetic prudential argument. *Patientes vincunt*, those who suffer win,[12] is true of Grisilde, of Prudence, and of all the women, not excluding Alice of Bath, who, though she claims to scorn patience, wins only when her husband strikes her to the ground.[13]

January's idealism is expressed in a series of shifting ways: in his marrying for vain theoretical reasons and holding a council on the subject, in the "fantasyes" the Merchant reports (E1577-1610), in the building of the garden as an image of the paradise he conceives marriage to be, in his blindness and what it symbolizes, in his "outrageous" jealousy. May is earthy and realistic in her interest in money, in her privy response to Damian, in general in the straightforward practical way in which she makes her arrangements with Damian. And, thanks to Proserpine, she has the words to "bear her husband on hand."

The scene between Pluto and Proserpine, along with what follows it, is the major explicit treatment in the *Canterbury Tales* of the differences between men and women, and deserves careful analysis. One and many are united here as the same opposition between man and woman is played out thrice, on four levels: mythic (Pluto and Proserpine), historic (Solomon and his wives), fictive (January and May), and "real" (Herry Bailly and Goodelief).

Before Pluto speaks we are reminded of that archetypal expression of male dominance, the rape: he "ravysshed" Proserpine "whil that she gadered floures in the mede," and fetched her away in his "grisely carte" (E2233). From Pluto we learn, on Solomon's authority, that men are good and women untrue (E2237-49). As Pluto says this he acts like a man, generalizing his experience by reference to authority.[14] He makes a learned statement, and promises to give January his sight so that he too will become a knower, not only of May but of all women: "Thanne shal he knowen al hir harlotrye, / Bothe in repreve of hire and othere mo" (E2263). We may compare January's search for a wife to Solomon's search "among a thousand women"; but, unlike Solomon, January thought he had found one good. Pluto aims to match January's knowledge to Solomon's by letting him see that none were good.

Proserpine replies that to May, and to "alle wommen after," she shall give "suffisant answere," a "face bold" to "bere hem doun that wolde hem accuse":

67

Al hadde man seyn a thyng with bothe his eyen,
Yit shal we wommen visage it hardily,
And wepe, and swere, and chide subtilly,
So that ye men shul been as lewed as gees.   (E2275)

Women's "face" and "visaging" will overcome men's "sight,"
that is, the "outer" male sense of sight or objective perception
will be stared down by an "inner" female sense of creative
insight and will power.[15] This is itself an aspect of female
"untruth": women not only are unfaithful to their husbands
but disregard objective truth. Similarly, various sub-rational
modes of speech—weeping, swearing, chiding—give
women a subtlety that renders men with all their knowing
"lewed" in comparison.[16] "Subtilly" is a key word here, since
subtlety is the province of clerks. Proserpine answers Pluto's
emphasis on authority and knowledge by asserting, and in the
process exhibiting, as the Wife of Bath does, a female brand
of scholarship, derived not from books but from inner nature
and, presumably, experience. Thus the difference between
men and women is ultimately epistemological, a matter of
different ways of knowing, different sources of knowledge,
and different attitudes to knowledge. In general, men learn
through authority, women through experience.

This difference is evident in another way: Pluto has made a
general statement about women, and has promised to give
one man knowledge of all women; Proserpine does not reply
with a generalization about men (as if knowing about them
were irrelevant), but promises to give May and all women the
power of bold-faced speech. Here as elsewhere, though both
sexes are being treated generally, women are treated at a
higher level of generalization. One may conclude from the
passage that in the world of the poem men rely on knowledge, women on intuition, but the source of knowledge will
vary from man to man, whereas the source of intuition is
female nature itself (passed down from generation to generation, as the Wife relies on "my dames loore" [D583] and as
Proserpine here swears "by my modres sires soule [E2265]).

In the light of this passage, the statement "boold was hir face" in the portrait of the Wife must be counted among her most basic generic characteristics, and her deafness may well suggest her disdain, not only for listening to Jankyn's reading, but for any knowledge derived from sense perception. She has knowledge, but it is experiential and unpredictable ("she koude muche of wandrynge by the weye"), and intuitive or traditional ("she koude of that art the olde daunce"); it makes her ready of speech ("in felaweshipe wel koude she laughe and carpe"). The word "koude" in its absolute sense "knew" is not used of the Parson. He is "a lerned man, a clerk," and his knowledge comes chiefly or even exclusively from a book, "Cristes gospel"; it finds expression not in "carping" but in teaching. His very manner of living is authoritative: he is an "ensample" to "lewed men," and he speaks naturally in "figure," the language of scholars.

The distinction also results in a broader range of degrees of knowledge for men. Men can be very learned like the Parson or the Clerk or Chauntecleer, or very wise and capable like Theseus or Arveragus, or very clever like Nicholas or the squire in the Summoner's Tale—but they can also be foolish or stupid or ineffective, despite what they know, like Absolon or Symkyn or the Friar's summoner or the Summoner's friar. Indeed virtually every man in the poem, including Theseus, has the value of his knowledge called into question at some point. Women (except perhaps for Prudence and Cecilia) do not reach heights of wise governance or book learning, but on the other hand there is no truly stupid woman in the poem. Custance's mothers-in-law are very wicked but not stupid; the woman in the Shipman's Tale is momentarily fooled by the monk, as May is here by Pluto, but like May has "face" and "suffisant answere" when the moment of realization comes.[17]

Proserpine goes on to display further female characteristics. Her response to Pluto's "auctoritees" is an example of "subtle chiding": she cleverly avoids the fact of May's untruth by citing (without specifying them) "many another man"

69

than Solomon who has found women true, by insisting in a clerkish way on Solomon's "sentence," and above all by launching a personal attack on Solomon for his lechery and idolatry. "I shal nat spare," she says, "to speke hym harm that wolde us vileynye" (E2310). In short, she "visages" both Solomon and Pluto, and gains the maistrie over the latter, who answers, "be no lenger wrooth; / I yeve it up!" (E2312). Like Chauntecleer and Jankyn he cannot bear to have his wife angry with him.

January and May then replay this scene with exactitude, though January does not extend his accusation to all women. January accuses briefly, May answers at length. May swears and chides subtly and faces down his sight, even in effect weeping ("'Allas,' quod she, 'that evere I was so kynde!'" [E2389]), and wins the maistrie: January "gives it up." She displays incidentally another standard female trait: healing by home remedy. This is a "remedy of love," like those Alice "knew per chaunce," in contrast to those of that other learned man juxtaposed to her in the General Prologue, the Doctor of Physic. Pertelote is a great offerer of home remedies; Alison heals Absolon of his malady (A3757), Prudence and Grisilde heal their husbands of their eccentricities; Canacee's ring enables her to know every herb, "and whom it wol do boote" (F154).

Though January has refrained from generalizing, Herry Bailly does it for him as soon as the tale is over:

Lo, whiche sleightes and subtilitees
In wommen been! for ay as bisy as bees
Been they, us sely men for to deceyve,
And from a sooth evere wol they weyve;
By this Marchauntes tale it preveth weel.   (E2425)

Herry is perhaps also generalizing for the Merchant, who does not state this point but who surely intends it. January's company in his misery finally includes five men: Adam, Pluto, Solomon, the Host, and the Merchant. The Host, of course, excepts his wife from the charge of untruth: she is true as steel; yet she is "a labbyng shrewe" and "hath an heep of vices mo" (E2429) (one is reminded of the unspecified "hye malice" of which the Merchant accuses his wife in his prologue [E1222]). Thus Goodelief hardly escapes the general charge; without being untrue to Herry, she can "twist him sore," as the Wife does to her fourth husband (D494). In short, the Merchant's Tale is a *locus classicus* of Chaucer's use of sexual stereotypes: it makes a series of statements about women and presents four very similar shrewish wives (the Merchant's wife, May, Proserpine, and Goodelief—with Solomon's harem and Eve hovering in the background); it makes no statements about men but implies several, and presents six very slightly differentiated defeated husbands (the Merchant, January, Pluto, the Host, Adam, and Solomon).

There are several ways in which Chaucer's treatment of sexual stereotypes furthers the presentation of one and many. The major way is that the individuating characteristics of various people are undermined by or subordinated to the characteristics of their sex: the many are seen to be reducible to two. This is not, of course, perfectly plain; in every case there is a certain interplay among the individual, the sex, and intermediate categories such as men's professions or asexual categories such as age. But the sexual stereotypes, particularly those of women, seem powerful enough to weight the balance toward such reduction.[18] And always flitting about the division into two sexes is the idea of professionalism, alternately supporting the division (men are professional, women domestic) and ironically effacing it (women are professional after all).

The second way arises from the reduction to two and not one. There is as much emphasis on the difference between men and women as on the similarities among men or among women. Sexual characteristics are an agent of unity only up to a point: finally they make for disunion (if not for multiplicity) because two such different sexes find it hard to coexist peacefully. Marriage, says the authority Saint Paul, makes the

71

The One and the Many

two one flesh (cf. RvT, A4197, of Aleyn and Malin: "they
were at oon"), but the experience rendered in the tales
suggests that otherwise it drives the two apart. As the Merchant says, with sharp irony:

> So buxom and so vertuous is she,
> They moste nedes lyve in unitee.
> O flessh they been, and o flessh, as I gesse,
> Hath but oon herte, in wele and in distresse.   (E1336)

Thus the well-recognized theme of marriage is best seen as
itself subordinate to the larger theme of the relationship of
one and many. Marriage is the major arena in life and in the
poem in which a strong attempt is made to forge diverse
elements into a unity.

I need not dwell long on the subject of marriage, since it has
been treated by so many authorities since Kittredge, and
since I have been touching on it implicitly throughout this
chapter. Chaucer's treatment of marriage shows about the
same balance of unity and multiplicity as most other aspects
of the poem show. It has a certain diversity, since every
marriage is in some way unique, but much that unifies. The
major source of unity is, paradoxically, an admission of
diversity: the implicit generalization that no marriage
achieves unity. Other subordinate or partial levels of generalization abound. A number of couples fail to achieve perfect
unity, or any unity at all, because of disparity of age: John and
Alison, January and May, the Wife and her first three husbands, the Wife and Jankyn. Others display the general
sexual dissimilitude: Walter and Grisilde, Chauntecleer and
Pertelote, Pluto and Proserpine, Melibee and Prudence, Dorigen and Arveragus. Some marriages founder on the wickedness of wives (or the gullibility of husbands): the marriage
between Symkyn and his wife, the marriage in the Cook's
Tale (probably), the marriage in the Shipman's Tale, Samson's and Hercules' marriages, Phebus's marriage, those of
the Merchant and the Host. The Wife's marriages, of course,

fall into all these classes. A fourth class is marriages doomed by the opposite cause, the saintliness of the wife: Custance and Alla, Cecilia and Valerian.

Of course words like "founder" and "doomed" are hyperboles. Only Phebus's marriage fails utterly, and many tales announce at the end the achievement of peaceful unity between spouses. This is even true of Alice and Jankyn and, by a hideous irony, of January and May. The disparity of age in the Wife's Tale is eliminated by magic. Melibee and Prudence, Walter and Grisilde, Pluto and Proserpine, and the merchant and his wife in the Shipman's Tale all reach agreement. In all these cases, however, the agreement comes about only when the wife gains the maistrie (I include Grisilde here since her patience seems a stronger force than Walter's various unilateral decisions, and is the ultimate victor). This is yet another classifying category, and puts all these agreements in the ironic light of capitulations or acknowledgements of dissimilitude. Cecilia's marriage belongs in this class also, except that Valerian's capitulation takes place near the beginning, and with little struggle. Custance's marriage to Alla falls prey at first to male professionalism: her troubles come because Alla is off at war. The last year of their marriage, after their reunion in Rome, is apparently peaceful enough, although Custance does not achieve the final peace she seeks until Alla dies and she returns to her father: "now is she scaped al hir aventure" (B1151).

Four marriages in the poem seem unequivocally good: those of Theseus and Ypolita, Palamon and Emily, the lord and lady at the end of the Summoner's Tale, and Dorigen and Arveragus. Of these I wish to discuss the first three briefly, the last in some detail. The presence and importance of the first three must simply be granted: they diversify the treatment of marriage in the poem by showing or suggesting that some marriages work. But they are certainly a minor voice in the argument. We see little of Ypolita; the marriage is there largely to round out Theseus in a human way, so that he has a home to govern as well as a dukedom, to explain Emily's presence, and perhaps also as symbolic of Theseus's right ordering of values: he "conquered al the regne of Femenye" (A866).[19] Emily and Palamon have a wedding rather than a marriage, and are also symbolic. So too the Summoner's lord and lady express a harmony in their town which the friar has disrupted. Nevertheless these symbolic marriages have a deep importance: the end of the Knight's Tale and the end of the Summoner's Tale are the two major un-ironic expressions, outside of the Parson's Prologue and Tale, of community and harmony in the poem, and it speaks well of marriage that it plays its role in the expression of this harmony.

Still, these places are brief and symbolic, not major episodes in Chaucer's treatment of marriage. The Franklin's Tale is traditionally thought of as the place where Chaucer has presented in full a fully harmonious marriage. If he has indeed done so, we must conclude that his treatment of marriage is diverse and at least partially hopeful, not uniformly skeptical; and my generalization that "no marriage achieves unity" cannot stand.

The Franklin's Tale purports to show that the stereotypes do not always apply: that a woman who is not a saint can have a firm devotion to an ideal of truth, and not demand maistrie, and that a man can avoid both harsh dominance like Walter's and meek compliance like January's or Jankyn's. Yet many readers have been uneasy with this interpretation,[20] whether because of the peculiar morality that impels Arveragus to honor Dorigen's rash vow, or because of the Franklin's shallow optimism and worship of his concept of "gentilesse," or because of the delicate unreality of the whole tale. I share this uneasiness, and I would like to suggest that it comes about very much from the power of the generic stereotypes, both of character and of plot, that operate everywhere in the poem. Dorigen is too like the typical woman, Arveragus too like the typical man, and the plot too like the typical plot.

The major issue is Dorigen. She seems to be an exceptional female of the Custance type, able to conceive of "trouthe" as an abstract ideal and hold firmly to it. There is no doubt that she loves Arveragus disinterestedly, is not a scold, and desires neither "maistrie" nor "suffisant answere." She is neither notably physical or material in her appetites like the Wife of Bath, nor is she attached like Grisilde to a monomaniac husband whose abstraction can give scope to her female capacity for patience and flexibility.

Nevertheless, certain central aspects of the female stereo-type emerge as the tale progresses. She is, first of all, forced to stay at home while her husband goes off in professional pursuit of worship and honor. Though she responds to this at first with a "male" extremeness—"Desir of his presence hir so destreyneth / That al this wyde world she set at noght" (F821)—she slides soon enough toward equanimity:

> By proces, as ye knowen everichoon,
> Men may so longe graven in a stoon
> Til som figure therinne emprented be.
> So longe han they conforted hire, til she
> Receyved hath, by hope and by resoun,
> The emprentyng of hire consolacioun,
> Thurgh which hir grete sorwe gan aswage;
> She may nat alwey duren in swich rage.   (F836)

This is perfectly sensible, of course; nor is she quite so open to impression as May: a stone is not wax. Yet there is flexibility here, a responsiveness to "process" and time that is very much like Alice's. And so her friends persuade her to "come and romen hire in compaignye" (F843; cf. the Wife, D543-62).

The prayer she utters about the rocks further compromises her original stony constancy. It is best seen in the context of Theseus's "firste moevere" speech (A2987-3040), that major passage in the poem (to be considered in detail in the next chapter), to which it forms a kind of "feminine" echo. Like Theseus, Dorigen reflects on God's "purveiaunce" and "gov-ernaunce," but to question, not affirm them:

> But, Lord, thise grisly feendly rokkes blake,

75

The One and the Many

> That semen rather a foul confusion
> Of werk than any fair creacion
> Of swich a parfit wys God and a stable,
> Why han ye wroght this werk unresonable?   (F872)

This question is reprehensible in the light of Theseus's demonstration that when the "moevere stable . . . and eterne" made the world, "wel wiste he why, and what therof he mente" (A3004, 2990), and amusing in relation to the emphasis in the poem on professional skill: God does his work badly, it says. It also calls into question the "suffraunce" toward her lord that she has promised in marriage: a fidelity toward her earthly lord that causes her to qualify her fidelity toward the Lord is incomplete and disordered. The question is further assailed within this tale by the later elaborate account of the relation of moon and tides on which the Orleans clerk relies to work his magic: that dependable relation is a function of what Theseus calls the "faire cheyne of love" (A2988, 2991). Though the clerk blasphemes by making use of his knowledge of the natural order to deceive, he is superior to Dorigen in his acknowledgement that that order exists, as she implies here:

> I woot wel clerkes wol seyn as hem leste,
> By argumentz, that al is for the beste,
> Though I ne kan the causes nat yknowe.
> But thilke God that made wynd to blowe
> As kepe my lord! this my conclusion.
> To clerkes lete I al disputison.   (F890)

In placing herself in opposition to clerks, the quintessential learned males, she aligns herself firmly with the Wife, with Pertelote, with Proserpine.[21] She does so also by throwing up rational argument in favor of the prayer "as kepe my lord," a "conclusion" that does not conclude. And her wish that the rocks might disappear is her version of female "visaging": faced with "sight," she responds, like May, by facing it down.

The whole speech is emotional and unschooled; it finds its impetus from within, from her feelings and desires, not from without: "visage" outdoes "sight." Her friends remove her from sight of the rocks into the manifest false paradise of the garden. Here she "let[s] hir sorwe slyde" (F924), and here the tempter enters in the form of the squire Aurelius, languishing "as a furye dooth in helle" (F950). Unlike Eve and May, of course, she resists the temptation, but once again lets her constancy slide a little, adjusts flexibly to the situation, rather amusingly. Having just assured Aurelius that she has made her "fynal answere" to him, she adds "in pley" her unfortunate rash promise, "syn I yow se so pitously complayne" (F991). Why she does this is debatable; above all it is a function of her love for Arveragus—she can't get the rocks off her mind—yet it seems also due to a misplaced "wommanly pitee" or a sudden urge to play again toward Aurelius the "daungerous" role she once played toward Arveragus when he wooed her, the role of the courtly lady imposing an impossible task. Whatever the cause, and however unpredictable the unfortunate result, one must find in the promise some compromise of her ideal of truth, some evidence of a sliding heart. This willingness she shows to toy playfully with the language, if not the fact, of infidelity is sharply contrasted with Arveragus's absolute faith:

No thyng list hym to been ymaginatyf,
If any wight hadde spoke, whil he was oute,
To hire of love; he hadde of it no doute.　　　(F1096)

His blissful ignorance, in its mild way, puts him in the company of blind cuckolds like January and John the Carpenter, or of the Miller:

An housbonde shal nat been inquisityf
Of Goddes pryvetee, nor of his wyf.
So he may fynde Goddes foyson there,
Of the remenant nedeth nat enquere.　　　(A3166)

Likewise Dorigen, in her mild way, follows the pattern of Alison, who first responds to Nicholas's advances by springing away "as a colt dooth in the trave" (A3282), then listens further, then grants him her love. The story has, indeed, taken on a fabliau-like pattern. In the absence of her husband the wife is subjected to the advances of a squire. She turns him away but not without leaving room for ingenuity, which he exercises, not in his own person but by hiring a clerk. It is as if she had Damian and Nicholas in league to pursue her. When in effect her love is evaluated at a thousand pounds, the venal bourgeois values of the Shipman's Tale have entered also, even if Dorigen does not know it. The marriage is genuinely threatened, and threatened in ways that have become typical in the poem: by the husband's professional absence; by the wife's irrationality, roaming, playfulness; by the presence of the squire as Satan in the garden; by the classic opposition of woman and clerk; by the whole "professional" interplay among representatives of four groups—knights, squires, clerks, wives.

The ending is extremely complex, and hard to interpret. It may very well be best to take it at its face value; in this case one must say that Chaucer draws on the stereotypes of plot and character only to grant greater value to the way they are transcended in the denouement. But if one supposes that their ironic power is not transcended, the ending appears in a whole new light. One way to see it is this: Arveragus, so far from abandoning maistrie, treats his wife as a possession to be shared or not shared. His generosity consists in sharing her. As a possession, she becomes a pawn in a professional competition of "quiting" among knight, squire, and clerk, not essentially different from that among carpenter, university clerk, and parish clerk in the Miller's Tale; or miller and clerks in the Reeve's Tale; or Knight, Miller, and Reeve in their competitive and professionally oriented tale-telling. The special twist is that the competition is based on generosity instead of aggressive selfishness, but the point is still competitive and professional, and leaves issues such as marriage and womanhood behind.

The ending may also be seen as a typical granting of maistrie to the woman. One possible way for Arveragus to respond—in Pauline (or Robertsonian) theology, the only right way—is to rule that Dorigen's promise is trivial in relation to the marriage vow, and should simply be disregarded. This is what the "heep" of listeners expects (F1493). But in fact such an assumption of maistrie would be extremely impractical, both because it would leave Aurelius in a pickle with the clerk, and because Dorigen, I submit, would obstinately refuse to accept it: though she cares for her husband she is also clearly, like Criseyde, her own woman. When instead Arveragus commands her to fulfil her promise, he is in fact granting her maistrie despite the appearance of command. Since it is clear that to her the choice is to fulfil her promise or die, and since it is further clear that she has no interest in dying, he is in effect letting her choose, as the knight does in the Wife of Bath's Tale. In telling her to fulfil her promise, he is saying, in effect, "Act independently of me. Do what your promise requires without regard to what you owe me." He actually releases her from her marriage vow (for just this once, of course), which is a significant loss of maistrie.

As in the other tales, this male yielding generates harmony, though only by a series of steps, a kind of domino effect of further acts of submission: for all her refusal of maistrie—or perhaps by means of it—Dorigen ends up having gained the upper hand over both Arveragus and Aurelius. It is important to see further that Aurelius's and the clerk's generous acts are not due solely to Arvaragus's. It is also Dorigen's "lamentacioun," her touching

> "Unto the gardyn, as myn housbond bad,
> My trouthe for to holde, allas! allas!" (F1513)

that makes the pity run in Aurelius's gentle heart. As he reports to the clerk, "the sorwe of Dorigen" made him "han of hire so greet pitee" (F1598, 1603). Proserpine's promise to all women extends to Dorigen as well as to May: she finds the words and the weeping to get her out of the "trappe" (F1341). I do not take it that these subversive patterns undermine the ideals the Franklin expresses. But they do moderate them, just as Dorigen's amiable weaknesses obviously moderate her high ideal of truth. They call attention to the great fictive distance from the reality that this "Breton lay" has. Rather than say that the Franklin's Tale resolves the issue of maistrie or balances the cynicism of the Merchant's Tale, it seems better to say that it offers a balance within itself—a balance wherein the particular account of a good marriage, an achieved unity, is qualified by various general associations: the partners are associated with the sterotypes of their sex, which are in conflict with each other; and therefore the marriage is associated with the typical marriage, which is purgatorial at best, and certainly not paradise.

I have tried in this chapter to show that a major mediation between one and many in the poem is its treatment of the sexes. Chaucer works constantly with a typical set of male qualities and a typical set of female qualities. Since such stereotyping undermines individuality, it is clearly a force for unity; but since the two sets of qualities are set against one another, that is, since the two sexes are so sharply differentiated, and seen as constantly in conflict, the treatment of the sexes is also an acknowledgment of multiplicity, of the impossibility of making many one.

Because their professional opportunities are more varied, the treatment of men has a greater superficial variety than the treatment of women. Thus there are far more men than women on the pilgrimage, and thus the poem contains very many more generalizations about women than about men. These generalizations suggest that there is also a certain superficial variety in women: women are either very saintly or very wicked. Nevertheless, the typical man is, like the Parson, caught in the grip of an idea; the typical woman is, like the Wife, solid, practical, earthbound. The ending of the

Merchant's Tale, including the conversations between Pluto and Proserpine and January and May and the remarks of the Host, is the fullest explicit treatment in the poem of the differences between men and women; it plays out with full explicitness the generic contrasts discernible in the opposed portraits of the Parson and the Wife and in a series of other couples.

Marriage is thus clearly a one-and-many theme, not only because the poem suggests that any one marriage merely repeats the age-old clash of the sexes, but because it is itself an attempt to make one of two, to create a new unity from irreconcilable opposites. The poem implies that that attempt usually fails; though in many marriages in the tales—more than are usually recognized—a certain peace is reached when the supremacy of the wife is established, this is a false unity, an ironic acknowledgment of dissimilitude, since it is achieved as it were by turning the husband into a cipher. There are, however, several happy marriages, briefly treated, which have clear positive force as expressions of unity. Most notable among these are the wedding at the end of the Knight's Tale and the marriage between the lord and lady glimpsed at the end of the Summoner's Tale. The Franklin's Tale may appear to present a harmonious marriage, but an examination of how the sexual and professional stereotypes work in it reveals a fabliau-like pattern, and a subtle struggle for maistrie, that support the sense of superficiality that others, on other considerations, have found in it.

Chaucer's treatment of sex and marriage suggests that we are one where we would prefer to be many—all men are alike, all women are alike, all marriages are alike—and divided where we would prefer to be unified—in marriage. Marriage is a thrust toward unity that still leaves us mired in multiplicity. If the pilgrims, or the reader, or Chaucer, are to find a source of genuine unity, they must look elsewhere.

4. Experience and Authority

Authority is related to experience as one to many.[1] Authority codifies the general experience of men, and treats it in a unified and unifying way, without allowing for individual exceptions. It takes its origin, of course, in the many, in the multitude of individual experiences of particular people; but it perceives them as one. Thus "Cato," for example, observing that marriages between people of similar age and estate work, and that other marriages between dissimilar people are troublesome, issues the dictum that "men sholde wedde his simylitude" (MillT, A3228)—a doubly unified statement, since in addition to exhibiting the unifying properties of all general rules, it is *about* unity: wedding, or unifying, should be itself based on unity or similitude. The wise man sees that he is like others and so accepts authority (or else he accepts authority first, which makes him like others); he marries somebody like him and is happy. The foolish man like John the carpenter asserts his uniqueness by marrying someone unlike him, and is unhappy—and his unhappiness validates the proverb. Of course the assertion of uniqueness may be unconscious, a mere product of ignorance of the authorities: John "knew nat Catoun, for his wit was rude" (A3227); the result is that he learns by bitter experience what he might have learned in school. But even when the assertion of uniqueness is conscious, as, say, Walter's is when he marries Grisilde—we may assume he knew his Cato—some larger ignorance is still evident, and Walter too learns the truth of the proverb through bitter experience. (It is true, of course, that he and Grisilde finally achieve happiness, but only after he has learned to become her similitude in wisdom and patience, and has discovered her innate nobility.)

This pattern operates repeatedly in the poem: an individual character chooses some course of action ("experience") which violates some general or proverbial truth ("authority"), and finds that his experience vindicates the truth: his experience is therefore authoritative, and he himself becomes, unwittingly, an "authority" in the sense that he is a living exemplum. This happens most obviously to the Canon's Yeoman, the Wife of Bath, Chauntecleer, Melibee, and to all those who enter an unequal marriage. But there are other examples: the Pardoner's three revelers, for instance, for whom *cupiditas* is indeed *radix malorum*, and over whom death, that grim exponent of "the way things are," establishes his authority; or Symkyn in the Reeve's Tale, who ignores not only what the Monk calls "swich gerdoun as bilongeth unto pryde" (B3820), but the Reeve's "hym thar nat wene wel that yvele dooth" (A4320), Aleyn's "ther is a lawe that says thus, / That gif a man in a point be agreved, / That in another he sal be releved" (A4182), and even Nicholas's "A clerk hadde litherly biset his whyle / But if he koude a carpenter bigyle" (A3300), which the Reeve makes clear applies to millers as well. We may see the authority of professional conventions operating here too. Symkyn thinks he can outwit clerks:

> They wene that no man may hem bigyle,
> But by my thrift, yet shal I blere hir eye,
> For al the sleighte in hir philosophye.
> The moore queynte crekes that they make,
> The moore wol I stele whan I take.
> In stede of flour yet wol I yeve hem bren.
> "The grettest clerkes been noght wisest men." (A4054)

But wit is the property of clerks, who "ben ful subtile and ful

queynte" (A3275), as the story shows. Such vindication of
proverbial truths is a major way in which the poem sets limits
on multiplicity.

The matter is more complex than this, however. In the first
place, the authorities themselves disagree, as Melibee and
Pertelote discover, or display a division between what they
say and what they do (e.g. the Summoner's friar or the judge
Apius in the Physician's Tale); and the very multiplicity of
conflicting proverbs in the poem—the Reeve's Tale is a good
example—suggests that authority is anything but one. Furthermore, the tales present enough conflicting experience to
raise direct questions about the validity of certain proverbs.
To take Cato's dictum once again: the poem may seem to
bear it out utterly, but in actuality questions it in two ways.
Since so many marriages succeed only when one partner
achieves the upper hand, the suggestion is that a basic dissimilitude of temperament is essential. Even more deeply,
the poem raises the question whether it is ever possible to
wed your similitude: men and women are too different, as
even such an apparently equal marriage as that of Averagus
and Dorigen shows. The poem seems to present through
experience some higher and more skeptical generalization,
that no true marriage is possible, or even that, in this world,
no true unity is possible.

Symkyn's adage, "the grettest clerkes been noght wisest
men," has a similar deep ambivalence. It is one of the central
maxims of the poem, a kind of experiencer's credo, sub-
scribed to by, among others, the Wife, the Summoner, the
Manciple (vis-a-vis the lawyers who employ him), and the
Canon's Yeoman. It is a home truth that corresponds to the
general exposure of male intellectual pretensions, or to Proserpine's derisive account of the unwisdom of Solomon the
wise. And yet it is also clearly a smug excuse for ignorance,
itself exposed not only in the Reeve's Tale but in the general
vindication of authority the poem so clearly displays; nor
does it seem to me to impugn the wisdom either of such
"authoritative" tales as the Knight's, the Parson's, or *Melibee*,

or of the poem's ultimate authority, the author. What in fact seems to be true is that though the poem most characteristically regards authority as a sounder source of knowledge and wisdom than experience, it also exposes certain falsities and weaknesses in authority—and so creates a vacuum to be filled by some third source of wisdom which transcends both.

I wish now to examine carefully several tales in which the issue of experience and authority is central: the Knight's Tale, the Monk's and Nuns' Priest's Tales, and *Melibee*. I shall not discuss the Wife's Prologue, central though that is to the subject; the reader will find in my earlier account of it under the rubric of professionalism a number of considerations clearly relevant to the present issue.[2] I reserve treatment of the Canon's Yeoman's and Parson's Tales, also central documents for this theme, for later chapters.

The first conjunction of the words "experience" and "auctoritee" in the poem seems innocuous enough, even vacuous. It comes as an apparent slackening in the sustained intensity of Theseus's speech, near the end of the Knight's Tale, on the "firste moevere" and the "cheyne of love." Having asserted that the universe is ordered by the limitation of the elements in space and of "engendred" things in time, Theseus supports (or interrupts) his assertion by remarking,

> Ther nedeth noon auctoritee t'allegge.
> For it is preeved by experience,
> But that me list declaren my sentence.   (A3002)

The lines at first glance seem a mere pause for breath, into which is inserted the commonplace of experience and authority, unnecessary to Theseus's grand exposition of his theme. The third line reads like an awkward apology for the commonplace or even for the entire speech: "all this is likely to be perfectly clear to all of you from your experience; it is just that I feel the urge to say what is on my mind." That is an odd admission from Theseus, accustomed as he is to public speaking, and to saying and doing what he likes out of a deep confidence that what he says and does is right. Theseus need not allege authority because he *is* authority; he can elucidate experience because he is very experienced. The lines suggest a sudden loss of his customary aplomb, as if he were speaking not so much to instruct others as to work out in words the meaning of his own experience.

Actually, however, that loss is not so sudden, for the speech has emerged slowly enough from Theseus's breast:

> Whan they were set, and hust was al the place,
> And Theseus abiden hath a space
> Er any word cam fram his wise brest,
> His eyen sette he ther as was his lest,
> And with a sad visage he siked stille,
> And after that right thus he seyde his wille.   (A2986)

"Seyde his wille": in view of the abiding and the quiet sigh, this seems not to mean "pronounced the royal will," but rather "spoke as his desire moved him."

The ultimate desire that moves him, of course, the final "sentence" he wishes to declare, is the desire to reestablish order and joy by marrying Emily to Palamon. But he arrives at the expression of that desire by such a circuitous route that one must feel his first desire is to reestablish order and joy in himself by articulating his sense of his own experience, and particularly the experience he has undergone in the poem.

That Theseus undergoes an experience, and learns something from it, is perhaps surprising, but demonstrable. There is no question that he enters the tale as a fully experienced man, a man who has conquered not just the "regne of Femenye" (A866) but "the Mynotaur, which that he wan in Crete" (A980), who has been to hell to seek Perotheus (A1200), who acts swiftly and magisterially to overthrow Creon. He is indeed the Theseus of myth, of "olde bookes," the possessor of the fullest possible range of experience in both war and love (though his "grete untrouthe of love" toward Ariadne, of which Chaucer gives the account in the *Legend of Good Women,* is here overlooked). Throughout the tale he is clearly the human counterpart of Jupiter. And yet he learns in the course of the tale. The first step in his learning process occurs at the end of the second part, when he has caught Palamon and Arcite fighting. He sentences them to death with characteristic swiftness, then reconsiders when the women urge mercy. He is perhaps here merely enacting further his mythic character, which is always susceptible to females; but Chaucer's presentation of the process is rationalized:

> He hath considered shortly, in a clause,
> The trespas of hem bothe, and eek the cause,
> And although that his ire hir gilt accused,
> Yet in his resoun he hem bothe excused,
> As thus: he thoghte wel that every man
> Wol helpe hymself in love.
> . . . .
> And in his gentil herte he thoughte anon,
> And softe unto hymself he seyde, "Fy
> Upon a lord that wol have no mercy,
> But been a leon, bothe in word and dede,
> To hem that been in repentaunce and drede,
> As wel as to a proud despitous man
> That wol mayntene that he first bigan.
> That lord hath litel of discrecioun,
> That in swich cas kan no divisioun,
> But weyeth pride and humblesse after oon." (A1768;
> 1781)

This is an interesting combination of general and particular. First he generalizes: every man will help himself in love (and therefore Palamon and Arcite should not be singled out for particular punishment). Then he particularizes: pride and humility differ, and cannot be treated the same.

But the real source of his mercy is not these "authoritative" reasonable maxims; it is an act of personal memory, engendered by an amused account of the god of love:

"But all moot ben assayed, hoot and coold;
A man moot been a fool, or yong or oold,
I woot it by myself ful yore agon,
For in my tyme a servant was I oon.
And therfore, syn I knowe of loves peyne,
And woot how soore it kan a man distreyne,
As he that hath ben caught ofte in his laas,
I yow foryeve al hoolly this trespaas."   (A1818)

It is out of his own experience that Theseus finds forgiveness; but the act of finding that forgiveness through memory is itself an experience, and, one feels, a new experience; he has not been given until now to such reflectiveness, or to changing his mind. This passage is perhaps best seen as a sort of rehearsal for the "firste moevere" speech. Both speeches are preceded by reflection, though here the reflections are spelled out for us, they are "short," and when they pass he looks up with "eyen lighte" (A1783) (not "sad visage"). Both begin with the actions of a god: here Cupid, there Jupiter. In both, the gods set limits on men; the "laas" in which Cupid catches lovers is a minor emblem of "this foule prisoun of this lyf" (A3061). Both lead Theseus to the resolution of a difficulty.

Ironically, however, the present resolution turns out to be inadequate, and to lead to the greater difficulty: the tournament he decrees here will lead to Arcite's death. Theseus resolves this first difficulty with an easy air of good humor. The moment of memory is genial; it prompts him without jarring him. He is confident that the tournament will solve everything safely. Later, to ensure that safety further, he places limits on the weapons to be used. Throughout he trusts fully his ability to conduct the tournament effectively. Even Arcite's injury does not upset him; he coolly conducts the post-tournament arrangements "as was right" (A2718).

He is deeply touched, however, when Arcite dies: "no man

89

myghte gladen" him (A2837). This is apparently a new experience for him, this sudden accidental death in the face of all his precautions, as is confirmed by what follows:

> No man myghte gladen Theseus,
> Savynge his olde fader Egeus,
> That knew this worldes transmutacioun,
> As he hadde seyn it up and doun,
> Joye after wo, and wo after gladnesse,
> And shewed hem ensample and liknesse.   (A2842)

Egeus has more experience than Theseus, or anyone else: he shows them "liknesse," that is, presumably, other cases in his experience like Arcite's; the result is that it loses its particularity and becomes part of the general phenomenon of "transmutacioun."

The small portion of Egeus's "muchel" speaking which is quoted for us is trite, but purposely so. The larger one's experience, the less likely one is to be original, the less need one has to be imaginative. Egeus has the flatness of an "auctoritee." Obviously, too, Chaucer cannot afford to allow Egeus to enter here with any final or personally felt wisdom. In the economy of the story, Palamon's and Arcite's private, too narrow experience is balanced by Egeus's broad generalizations.[3] Theseus, eventually, must combine Egeus's breadth of knowledge with Palamon's and Arcite's youthful ability to suffer new experience with private pain. Another way to describe the relationship is to say that as Theseus responds calmly to Palamon's and Arcite's painful experience of love, Egeus responds calmly to Theseus's painful experience of death. Events have placed Theseus here in the position Palamon and Arcite were in before; the focus of the story has shifted from them to him. Arcite, of course, is out of the way, but the shift can be seen in the fact that it is Theseus and not Palamon toward whom Egeus's consolatory wisdom is primarily directed. Theseus can speak with full authority at the end of the poem precisely because he has lived with full awareness and full personal response through the events of the poem. His final consoling speech works better than Egeus's because it has a pulse of individuality, it arises out of personal emotion and private contemplation. It is most effectively general and authoritative because it originates in particular experience.

Nevertheless, despite this balance in its origin, its message is firmly general. Men and things, "al that is engendred," are partial, corruptible, always in "progressioun"; God is "hool," i.e., One, perfect, stable. It is essential to notice the relation of Theseus's experience to these generalities: he defines God as whole, stable, and perfect because he has found not only Arcite but himself to have been partial (he saw in part when he thought he was seeing whole, he found his experience to be less "whole" than Egeus's, he found himself incomplete in his inability to be gladdened), unstable (i.e., capable of learning and growth), and imperfect (particularly in the imperfection of his solution to the rivalry between the lovers). The implicit comparison in the opening lines between God and himself is striking: Theseus has also moved a cause in the interest of love, with high intent and great effect; but he has discovered that he did not know fully well "what therof he mente." Again, he bound Palamon and Arcite, and established duration for them—but with a chain of public vengeance or at best justice, not love. One meaning of the proof by experience that God so acts is that Theseus has experienced such a pattern of action and intent on his own "godlike" level of authority.

His reflections have enabled him not only to define God but to define man and things, and this he does in a rigorous move toward generality. Things endure, and therefore find their fullest and most permanent identity, as species, as progressions, and by successions; that is, the real existence is not that of the individual but that of the species, which lives on as its individual members succeed and are succeeded by one another. Nor do men and women differ from things, or classes of men from each other; perhaps impelled by Egeus's examples of "liknesse," and no longer interested in the sort of "resoun" that makes "divisioun" between "pride and humblesse," Theseus gathers us all under the single rubric of death. But his view of the final utter unity of things does not stop there, with the experience of death. Finally all things will be one, as God converts "al unto his propre welle / From which it is dirryved" (A3038). Unity is the initial and the ultimate state; our multiple "progressions" (like Egeus's "pilgrimage") on earth are partial and therefore tentative. (The form of the *Canterbury Tales* imitates this state of things. The General Prologue and the Parson's Tale are general unified static wholes, in which time is muted or suspended; the tales in between them are a multiplicity of particular competing narratives, a world of flux. Every part derives from the whole of the General Prologue, "descendynge so til it be corrumpable" (A3010), until the Parson moves to "convert" the company into an image of the Celestial Jerusalem, "from which it is derived.")

Theseus concludes his drive toward unity in the expected way by binding Emily to Palamon in marriage. He once again imitates Jupiter, making, with high intent, a fair chain of love; that this binding is more gracious and fruitful than the chains with which he originally imprisoned Palamon and Arcite suggests what he has learned, as does his dictum to Emily that "gentil mercy oghte to passen right" (A3089). Like Jupiter "convertynge al unto his propre welle," he makes unity of multiplicity, a whole of two parts:

"I rede we make of sorwes two
O parfit joye, lastynge everemo."   (A3072)

This concludes his speech perfectly: the marriage itself, as "a thyng that parfit is and stable" (cf. A3009), will be a sign of the First Mover, just as, by a happy coincidence, the word for "one" is a sign of unity, a perfect circle. And yet certain ironies remain. Has not Theseus just proven that nothing earthly can last evermore, that all things are not perfect but "corrumpable"? Furthermore, though to make two into one may seem a godly "conversion," it may equally well be thought of as one more example of simple "progressioun," or of "this worldes transmutacioun"—an appropriate phrase from the Egeus passage just echoed in the line "but after wo I rede us to be merye" (A3068). Time governs the conclusion: the speech is a "longe serye," i.e., itself an example of "progressioun"; merriment is to come "after wo"; the marriage is to take place "er we departen." These remind us that the process of making one joy of two sorrows is also a progression in time and so corruptible. Has Theseus forgotten all he has learnt, and all he has just said?

Surely not; it is truer to the tale, I think, to regard him as making virtue of necessity all through the final scene. He has learned that his plans are subject to vicissitude; but this has taught him not to cease planning but only to plan as closely as possible in accordance with nature. This means for him to govern his state as Jupiter governs the world; thus he imitates Jupiter, but in a chastened, not an arrogant, spirit. The unity he creates, the perfection and lastingness he seeks to create, are surely partial, surely subject to succession; and yet such seeking has been proven to be as virtuous and necessary as the recognition that it will fail. Theseus has as whole a vision as it is possible for man to have. In arguing that he grows, I do not mean to deny either the far greater wholeness of vision he has throughout than Palamon, Arcite, or anyone else, or the depth of his understanding at the end. The tone of his last few paragraphs is complex. He has advertised merriment, and is merry, as in his needling of Palamon (and himself): "I trowe ther nedeth litel sermonyng / To make yow assente to this thyng" (A3092). But the merriment is neither forced and artificial nor ignorant and forgetful: his argument has brought him to the conclusion that he should be merry, and so he is merry, naturally and unselfconsciously; but his very merriment is humble, obedient, not an assertion of human self-sufficiency but an acceptance of such grace as Jupiter grants, which is enough. He knows the marriage will endure only "by successiouns," not in itself, but he accepts its value precisely because it is part of that series of successions, that chain of love. The perception here—on Theseus's part, on the Knight's, on Chaucer's—of the relation of the individual to the perfect whole is not unlike Homer's in his presentation of the scenes on Achilles' shield (another "O", like Theseus's stadium and the word for "one"), and the deep acceptance that accompanies that perception is also the same in both.

In view of all this one may argue that the center of interest in the Knight's Tale is indeed the philosophical question of the relation of part to whole. We are made to see how partial Palamon, Arcite, and Emily are; how whole in contrast is Theseus's vision of things. But the final depth comes when Theseus is made to see how partial his own vision has been, and yet must go on acting as if his vision were whole.

Theseus is whole in part because of his age. He is set between Egeus on the one hand and Palamon, Arcite, and Emily on the other, as—to cite Homer once more—in the *Odyssey* Odysseus is set between Laertes and Telemachus. The tale suggests that youthful experience is particular; young people like Palamon and Arcite think the world revolves around them, they are impressed by the uniqueness of their experience (and so cannot share it with each other). Old people like Egeus are the opposite; they have seen so much that they are impressed mainly by likeness. They see only generalities as the young see only particulars. This helps explain Egeus's triteness. Theseus is in the middle, old enough to see his youth in the integrating light of memory, but still young enough to feel (Egeus seems to have no feeling) and to learn. Part of his "perfection" comes from his standing between these extremes, balancing age and youth. One might say that Chaucer has combined in the Knight's main character a balanced view of youth and age that he presented analytically in the General Prologue in the portraits of Knight and Squire. E. Talbot Donaldson well says that "what the Squire is, the Knight once was, and what the Knight is, the Squire may yet be."[4] The Knight has grown away from particular accomplishments and accoutrements, away from the many of the physical to the one of the spiritual; but this one is not seen as better (except in that it is grown *toward*, is a goal) but as itself partial, part of a complex whole that combines both.

The Knight's Tale is an experiential tale which leads to an authoritative statement, a statement whose implications extend far beyond the experiences which occasion it, and which diminishes individual experience by deriving significance from the One. But the tale does not deny value altogether to experience, since the experiences which it embodies—and which give it literary life—engender value, and since the primary application of that value is to Theseus himself. The tale grants univocal validation neither to experience nor to authority, but suggests that the two sources of knowledge are deeply interdependent.[5]

Among the ways the Miller's Tale parodies the Knight's Tale is that, instead of working slowly from a set of experiences to an authoritative generalization, it takes as given certain general or proverbial statements: not only "men sholde wedde his simylitude," but "alwey the nye slye / Maketh the ferre leeve to be looth" (A3393) and "a clerk hadde litherly biset his whyle / But if he koude a carpenter bigyle" (A3300; a "professional" truth); perhaps also, for Absolon's revenge, "whil that iren is hoot, men sholden smyte" (*Melibee*, B2226). A further given is the set of characterizations. These seem particular, but are actually professional stereotypes which, along with the generalizations, operate like major premises, against which the minor premise of the events is placed, leading to a necessary conclusion. Thus, clerks must beguile carpenters; Nicholas is a clerk, John a carpenter; therefore Nicholas must beguile John. Or, Nicholas as a clerk is a loner, an intellectual, sly and "hende," and likes love; therefore, he operates alone, using his wits to stay slyly handy to Alison and win her love. The experience of the tale is foreordained ("purveyed"), not so much by Nicholas's providence or providing as by the proverbs and the stereotyped characterizations and professional conventions. The narrative is an enactment or imitation of a providential order, not in its subject matter and events but in its structure, and the enactment is not mysterious, as in the Knight's Tale, but logical, inevitable.[6] The slow pace of the Knight's Tale is a product of its tentativeness, its full and gradual presentation of a complex experience; the Miller's Tale is swift because of its narrator's utter confidence in the truth of his proverbs.

We can see a similar pairing in the Monk's Tale and the Nuns' Priest's Tale. The Monk's Tale has the look of authority to it: the authority of a genre, tragedy, with its regular pattern of movement from "hye prosperitee" to "meschaunce" and a wretched end, and the authority of a proverb: "whan that Fortune list to flee, / Ther may no man the cours of hire withholde" (B3186). Furthermore, the Monk makes one of many, by tending to reduce the individuality of his subjects in the service of his single tragic pattern. Nevertheless, certain major "experiential" elements remain. The poem here moves farthest from literary stereotypes; the Monk's Tale is the only place (unless we count such shadowy—and conventional— figures as Cecilia, Virginia, and Custance) wherein historical people appear. By treating separately a series of individual historical persons, the Monk implies that the individual person has dignity and importance. Furthermore, by ascribing causality to Fortune rather than to the "firste moevere," he seems to deny the "purveiaunce" which Theseus's experience has caused him to posit as the mark of authoritative governance. Indeed, Fortune or "what happens" is the emblem of experience throughout the poem: Fortune is to God as experience is to authority (and as woman is to man).

And even such authority and consistency as the Monk grants to Fortune is undermined, since he sometimes ascribes a moral purpose to her and sometimes does not.[7] He begins with falls activated morally: Lucifer "fel . . . for his synne" (B3192), Adam "for mysgovernaunce / Was dryve out" (A3203), Sampson made the patent error of telling his secret to his wife. Nebuchadnezzar and Balthasar earn their falls, as do Nero, Holofernes, Antiochus, and Croesus. But other falls, though explicable as the outcome of human animosity, are undeserved: these include the falls of Hercules, Caesar, Zenobia, Alexander, and all the "modern instances." In all these cases, the Monk can do nothing but rail at Fortune for falseness and caprice, or simply report that she brings men "out of joye . . . to sorwe" (B3588). In the last stanza he is allowed to pronounce, he claims that the purpose of tragedy is to bewail "that Fortune alwey wole assaille / With unwar strook the regnes that been proude" (B3954), once again granting Fortune a moral aim; but there are too many stories which do not support this claim. One story, Nebuchadnezzar's, does not even fit the existential definition of tragedy, since it ends happily.

Finally, despite the Monk's lame generalizations, one is impressed in many of the stories by the variety and power of "al this world of prees" (B3327) and by the strong human impulse to follow it, to establish one's own experience as primary. There is a wide range of experience here, from Nebuchadnezzar's bestial penance which earns him new understanding to Nero's crazed desire both to gain experience and destroy authority, figured in his slitting his mother's womb "to biholde / Where he conceyved was," and in the "greet grevaunce" he feels over having once been accustomed to rise in the presence of his teacher Seneca (B3675, 3703). The Monk's simple formulas do not solve the very problems of the relation of experience to authority that he himself, somewhat unconsciously, raises.

The Nuns' Priest answers him with the shrewdest and most profound exposition in the poem of the power of authority. He opposes the Monk's assumptions about individuality by being as reductive as possible, reductive of dignity and reductive of individuality: he brings men down to the level of chickens, and reduces character to the stereotypical forms of hen, cock, and fox. (Incidentally, he relegates several of the Monk's own tragedies, of Croesus, Nebuchadnezzar [through Daniel], and Nero, to the role of minor analogues.)

For the beast fable goes a step further than the fabliau in the presentation of authoritative stereotypes. The fabliau, as I have argued, relies generally on certain class distinctions and stereotypes of sex, age, and profession, and specifically on a set of slightly individuating characteristics presented as a premise in a set description at or near the beginning of the narrative. The beast fable can do without the second method entirely, and works with a system of stereotypes that is even more closed—much more closed—than that of the fabliaux. Fabliaux allow for some variation within a class. Though the clerks John and Aleyn in the Reeve's Tale share certain central attributes with the Miller's Nicholas (opposition to tradesmen, reliance on intelligence, sexual vigor and success), they are unlike him also in ways that are probably not entirely due to a stereotyped set of differences between Oxford men and Cambridge men. But animal stereotypes are far more rigid: the fox is always sly, the rooster always vain, the hen always a timorous domestic busybody. The Cambridge roosters act just like the Oxford roosters. This fits with observation: men readily perceive differences among themselves, but they certainly cannot tell one fox from another, and they probably cannot tell one hen from another; if they can differentiate among roosters, the basis on which they do so is quite superficial—and ironically seems the very basis of the besetting vanity of the roosters. That is, we sense that the rooster senses that he is important because he looks distinctive; but when all roosters cock and strut because they are different, the difference disappears, or matters only as a source of sameness. Animal stereotypes also carry greater authority than human professional stereotypes. One may argue, as the Reeve does, that not all carpenters are gullible; but no one will argue that not all foxes are sly. Thus the beast fable is the ultimate vehicle for the authoritative mode with its "behaviorist" view of character: the experience whose particulars it narrates is merely the inevitable unfolding of standard inner traits and proverbial truths.

A problem arises, however: if readers know and accept the

stereotypes, and if these are rigid and produce inevitable actions, what motivates the plot? Must there not be some uncertainty, some sense of various possibilities, to move events forward and maintain the reader's interest in them? And if there is, does that not imply that individual experience has some validity? Indeed, is it not a principle implicit in narrative literature that individual experience is valuable? The answer to these last three questions is, of course, yes. Plots require uncertainty, and uncertainty validates experience. An altogether authoritative esthetic would reduce stories to general statements. Conversely, of course, an altogether experiential esthetic would reduce stories to chronicles, chains of events with no discernible significance. Every narrative is more or less authoritative, more or less experiential. The Nuns' Priest's Tale has various experiential aspects. Perhaps the most basic is its trust that to hear or read the story is "an experience" for the reader: he forgets or suspends his full knowledge of the character conventions, so that he can follow the plot and the revelation of character traits with interest. The reader is by definition not an authority. That is the author's role; the reader's role, by default if nothing else, is to be uncertain, and to relieve that uncertainty by finding out what happens: to experience the plot. But that is not the only uncertainty, for another lurks in the clash of the stereotypes themselves. If the rooster's vanity implied only stupidity, surely we could expect the sly fox to outwit him (and we know that wit is the issue, since before the fox can put his superior strength to advantage, he must trick the rooster into not flying away). But in fact vanity must imply some intelligence after all, since it is a product of thought and self-reflectiveness, and of an incipient grasp of scope. In comparison to hens, the rooster has less common sense but more vision. Thus the story contains a conflict, either between the rooster's stupidity and his intelligence, or between the rooster's intelligence and the fox's. And conflict makes for uncertainty.

We can grant, then, a certain necessary ingredient of

experience in the tale. Furthermore, the Nuns' Priest plays this ingredient for all it is worth, spinning out the initial confrontation between Chauntecleer and Pertelote as if it were a necessary presentation of character, and delaying the denouement as long as possible so as to maintain suspense. In length, in articulacy, in elaboration it has all the surface appearance of an experiential tale. The Monk reduces a series of individual histories to a single brief formula, and tells many in a stanza or two; the Nuns' Priest mocks this by extending and articulating as far as he can what is in fact a stereotyped and predictable story.

What generalizations does the Nuns' Priest's Tale ratify? On the surface, it seems to be an elaborate exemplum, fuller even than the two that Chauntecleer gives, illustrating the generalization "dremes been to drede" (B4253).[8] Or it may seem to exemplify rather the proverbs

> he that wynketh, whan he sholde see,
> Al wilfully, God lat him nevere thee! (B4622)

and

> God yeve hym meschaunce,
> That is so undiscreet of governaunce
> That jangleth whan he sholde holde his pees. (B4625)

Or, to combine them, "keep your eyes open and your mouth shut." But surely the ratification of conventional wisdom goes deeper than these proverbs; they are relatively individual, by-products of the experience, the particular set of events. A deeper level of generalization lies in the ratification of the animal stereotypes, and a still deeper level in the application of those to men and women. Chickens, the tale says, are "chicken," i.e., timid; cocks are cocky, hens henpeck, foxes can outfox themselves. Nothing happens out of character; the tale corroborates our common understanding of things through the medium of the attributes we assign conventionally to animals.[9] But further, since those attributes are, after all, human attributes, it corroborates our sense of the typical in ourselves. This includes a number of separable generalizations: that we are basically animals; that we tend to overemphasize our importance; that like animals we are not very differentiated from individual to individual; that men are vain, pretentious, and too intellectual while women are domestic, scolding, and too earthy and small-minded; that experience is predictable, "purveyed" by deterministic forces both within and without ourselves. Most of these generalizations are reinforced still further by the hints that the plot is a replay of the story of Adam and Eve. Whether any reader in his ordinary character thinks these generalizations true is irrelevant; the tale asserts them, inexorably, and is persuasive about them at least as long as it casts its spell. Or even if one does not accept them even for a moment, one still must acknowledge that this is how the tale works, this is what it says. It is surely the deepest and most ambitious tale of authority, and to my mind it is the most persuasive and successful. The argument for authority was never presented more richly.

One way in which the poem unifies the many is that it presents the conflict between experience and authority, or the experiential and authoritative narrative modes, not only in pairs of tales such as the Knight's and the Miller's, or the Monk's and the Nuns' Priest's, or in individual tales like the Wife's Prologue, but in its whole self. It can be thought of, as I have argued in chapter 2, as a fabliau, moving confidently and expectedly from the generalizations and characterizations of the General Prologue, merely bearing out with a set of particulars what is implicit there: given this mixture of characters, this is what inevitably results. Such apparent surprises as develop in the links and in certain prologues (e.g., the Wife's and the Pardoner's) are actually embraced within this large expectation. Even the final surprise of the Retraction is implicit in the character of an author, particularly an

The One and the Many

author whose narrative investigations of experience so regularly vindicate authority.

Opposed to this "authoritative" pattern (or, perhaps, finally, corroborating it) is an "experiential" pattern like that of the Knight's Tale, in which all that the characters undergo, their confusing experience of multiplicity, leads to the Parson's Tale. As the General Prologue is to the whole what the portraits are to a fabliau like the Miller's, Reeve's, or Friar's Tale, so the Parson's Tale is to the whole what Theseus's speech is to the Knight's Tale: it articulates an interpretation of life that will enable the pilgrims, and the reader, to organize the confusion events have led to—though it would be going too far to suppose that the Parson's Tale is the product of his experience on the pilgrimage. Unlike Theseus, he could have told it at the start, though his *audience* would have been unready for it, as the Shipman's early objection to a tale from the Parson indicates. By the end, reader and pilgrim are ready to hear it, just as Emily and Palamon are ready to accept Theseus's speech, as they would not have been earlier. The tales provide the experience of "liknesse" that makes us accept the Parson's authority.

This initial discussion of experience and authority can be concluded with a brief analysis of a tale which in important ways both complements the Knight's Tale and anticipates the Parson's Tale: Chaucer's *Tale of Melibee*. Though line for line it contains more "auctoritees" than anything else in the *Canterbury Tales,* it actually follows an experiential pattern as the Knight's Tale does, and it makes (or implies) some central distinctions among authorities; it generates a specifically Christian ethic to complement the Knight's Boethian metaphysics.

Melibee is an experiencer: "thy name is Melibee, this is to seyn, 'a man that drynketh hony.' Thou hast ydronke so muchel hony of sweete temporel richesses, and delices and honours of this world, that thou art dronken" (B2601). His honey is the counterpart of the wine the Pardoner's revelers drink, or of the molten metals the Canon works with: all

102

represent the flow of experience, which is deceptive, as Prudence goes on to say, in "the wordes of Ovide": "Under the hony of the goodes of the body is hyd the venym that sleeth the soule" (B2605). The Pardoner's Tale makes this clear in action. Melibee is of course more like the Pardoner's revelers than like Alice or the Canon. He has not consciously and rebelliously chosen experience over authority, but simply drinks the cup placed before him. Like John in the Miller's Tale ignoring Cato, he has disobeyed a series of general tenets without realizing in the least that he is doing so. This very passiveness makes him ready enough to drink in authority when the cup is filled with proverbs; as he says to Prudence, Solomon "seith that 'wordes that ben spoken discreetly by ordinaunce been honycombes, for they yeve swetnesse to the soule and holsomnesse to the body.' And, wyf, by cause of thy sweete wordes, and eek for I have assayed and preved thy grete sapience and thy grete trouthe, I wol governe me by thy conseil in alle thyng" (B2304). Thus Melibee comes to learn the value of attending to authority; he "assays and proves" wisdom in the course of the tale, and presumably goes on afterwards to experience further the value of directing his life by authority.

A more interesting and subtler development occurs in Prudence. Like Theseus, she seems to take an authoritative stance from start to finish; but in fact she can be seen, like him, to learn and develop in the course of the tale. Thus to a certain extent she moves in the opposite direction from Melibee: he gains a new appreciation of authority, a new understanding of his relation to general ideas; she, by allowing a new set of experiences to change her, shows herself open not merely to proverbial summations of experience but to experience itself. She works out a philosophy. She clearly is not ready at the start of the tale to tell Melibee to forgive his enemies; rather, in the course of the arguments she brings up to him, she comes to see that that is the right course. The conviction she starts with is of the need to deliberate and take counsel; beyond her firm belief in this she has no answer; she herself needs the deliberation in order to see her way to the answer.

The change she experiences may be expressed as a development from a wholly prudential to a somewhat providential point of view. She frees herself from a set of merely ethical authorities and takes up with theological authorities; she moves her allegiance from a world governed by common sense to a world divinely ordered. This is a relative and rather bland movement, to be sure; she begins her advice, after all, by urging that Melibee take God as his counselor, and her trust in Providence at the end has a clear prudential cast. But in general her early advice is notably self-seeking and pusillanimous. The insistence on secrecy (B2328ff.), for example, on hiding your counsel in your heart from "any wight," friend or foe, because otherwise "he holdeth thee in his snare" is radically opposed to the whole communal spirit of the pilgrimage. She claims that true reconciliation is impossible: 'ne trust nat to hem to whiche thou hast had som tyme werre or enmytee" (B2374). She says that servants do not love their masters. She urges inactivity in preference to attempting something you are unsure you can complete. She is concerned constantly with "honour" and "profite." She claims that "men shal alwey fynde a gretter nombre of fooles than of wise men" (B2448). She approves the lawyers' principle that Melibee "over alle thyngs" should protect his person and guard his house (B2487), and Solomon's "weleful is he that of alle hath drede" (B2507). When she counsels prayer, it is prayer for self-protection (B2491). She says strangers should be held suspect:

And if so be that he falle into thy compaignye paraventure, withouten thyn assent, enquere thanne as subtilly as thou mayst of his conversacion, and of his lyf bifore, and feyne thy wey; sey that thou wolt go thider as thou wolt nat go; and if he bereth a spere, hoold thee on the right syde, and if he bere a swerd, hoold thee on the left syde.

(B2502)

This is hardly the principle followed by our "compaignye /
Of sondry folk, by aventure yfalle / In felaweshipe," and in
particular by the pilgrim who can say that "shortly, whan the
sonne was to reste, / So hadde I spoken with hem everichon /
That I was of hir felaweshipe anon." Nor is Prudence's
respectable self-protection at all consistent with the praise
rendered elsewhere in the poem to "sely" characters like
Custance or the "litel clergeon," who trust wholly to the
providence of God for their protection. One senses neither a
Christian cosmos nor a gospel ethic here.

But another strain runs through the tale, and gathers
strength toward the end. It seems to have a clear beginning in
Melibee's misunderstanding of the physicians' advice that
"oon contrarie is warisshed by another contrarie" (B2467). He
takes this to mean that, as his enemies have "doon [him] a
contrarie," i.e., assailed him, he should "doon hem another"
(B2470). Prudence shows it rather means that

> wikkednesse shal be warisshed by goodnesse, discord
> by accord, werre by pees, and so forth of othere thynges.
> And heerto accordeth Seint Paul the Apostle in manye
> places. He seith: "Ne yeldeth nat harm for harm, ne
> wikked speche for wikked speche; but do wel to hym
> that dooth thee harm, and blesse hym that seith to thee
> harm." And in manye othere places he amonesteth pees
> and accord.   (B2484)

Except for a brief admonition regarding wisdom from
Saint James, this is the first time since the opening paragraphs
of the tale that the New Testament has been quoted. A
development seems to be taking place that has a typological
aspect: Saint Paul (or the Christ of the Sermon on the Mount
whom Paul is quoting) replaces Solomon, completes his
wisdom by moving it from a secular to a religious realm.
Melibee is an "Old Testament" man: he wants an eye for an
eye. Prudence has countered this ethic first by counseling
deliberation, in the Solomonic manner; now the very process

of deliberation causes her to move out of the Old Testament mode altogether, to counter it with Christian pacifism. Solomon and his kind are not suddenly dropped, of course, but from this point on Prudence's arguments take on more and more of a theological air. Though "ther may no man comprehende ne serchen" the judgments of God sufficiently (B2597), she interprets the attack on their daughter as a just visitation on Melibee for his sinfulness. Saint Paul is quoted again to the effect that vengeance lies properly with God, and Prudence then turns to a lengthy praise of patient suffering (B2657-2708). This is supported, to be sure, by a rash of Solomons, but supported also by Gregory, James, Peter, and Paul, and by the examples of Christ and the saints, wherein, if a distinction can be made between patience and suffering, it is worth noting that the Solomonic dicta mention patience only, not suffering; the various Christian instances mostly deal explicitly with suffering.

All this groundwork makes Prudence's final counsel, "that ye accorde with youre adversaries and that ye have pees with hem" (B2865), perfectly reasonable when it comes, though certainly not what one could have predicted earlier, and of course quite a surprise to the thickheaded Melibee. She supports it with the Sermon on the Mount, the first time Christ himself is quoted directly. She urges Melibee to reconcile himself first with God, then with his enemies. A struggle on his part follows, and maneuvers on hers, but the end is finally achieved: he forgives his enemies completely. The Christian ethic triumphs. What has also implicitly come to reign is a providential in place of an experiential understanding of the universe. The acknowledgement that vengeance is God's, and that God may be trusted to carry it out mysteriously but justly, releases Melibee from the feeling that he must take it into his own hands. In the godlike act of forgiveness he expresses his confidence in God; like Theseus initiating a chain of love, he shows his trust in God by imitating him. He had earlier asserted that "Fortune hath norisshed me fro my childhode" (B2635); he now implicitly rejects that unstable goddess for a Lord he is certain will bring him to "the blisse that nevere hath ende" (B3078). Such a stable hope frees him to take the risk of forgiveness, a risk that is a far cry from the safe course of self-protection that Prudence had earlier been plumping for. Finally the tale opts for "seliness," as the Man of Law's Tale does.

The final paragraphs, indeed, seem to look forward, in their stress on repentance for sin, on forgiveness, on judgment and the Last Judgment, on the role of God as merciful judge, to the Parson's Tale and the Retraction. Melibee forgives "to this effect and to this ende that God of his endelees mercy wole at the tyme of oure diynge foryeven us oure giltes that we han trespassed to hym in this wrecched world" (B3074). So too Chaucer revokes his "enditynges of worldly vanitees," "that Crist have mercy on me and foryeve me my giltes . . . so that I may been oon of hem at the day of doom that shulle be saved" (I1092).

Thus *Melibee* seems to have as one purpose a kind of foreshadowing of the Parson's Tale. Despite its Christian conclusion, however, it maintains a certain prudential attitude and political dimension to the end. Forgiveness is, after all, the best policy; Prudence is never untrue to her name. In this light it might be seen as standing in a certain opposition to the Parson's Tale, a treatise of politic worldly conduct as against a treatise of personal moral conduct, how to get along in this world as opposed to how to get into the next. But the Christian ethic, and the emphasis on Melibee's personal salvation, are so strong at the end, and the Parson's Tale is itself so politic and prudential in its schema of personal salvation, that I think they are better seen as complementary rather than as opposed. One treats a single political issue, how to respond to an attack; the other treats the entire spectrum of personal moral action; but both arrive at the same vision of a moral universe ordered by God in which charitable action in the name of God is prudent for both secular and eternal purposes. *Melibee* is the subtler, more understated of the two; the proper one to put here in what is roughly the center of the poem (in the Bradshaw order, at least), because of its narrative dimension, its problematic, experiential mode (it takes a problem and develops an answer to it in a gradual process), its humor (Prudence wins the maistrie; *Melibee* is a "female" approach to the issues, the Parson's Tale a "male" approach), and its muted and delayed introduction of the ultimate issue of salvation. The Parson's Tale, coming at the end, rightly eschews the mode of *Melibee* for an open and thoroughgoing analysis from the start of the ultimate issue. But both finally take the same stand.

Melibee adds to experience and authority a third mode of knowledge: "seliness." Prudence is open to the experience of learning, to the new understanding that the application of her "auctoritees" to the situation gradually leads her to; but that new understanding is precisely that "seliness" is valuable. She undergoes an authoritative, or, as we would say, authentic experience that leads her to urge what Custance knows intuitively to be right: the innocent, vulnerable, unquestioning acceptance of the will of God. This leads to peace, which is unity.

5. Closure

I have dealt in the three preceding chapters with several thematic manifestations of the conflict of one and many, and argued or implied in all that the poem exhibits a thrust away from the many and toward the one, away from the particular and toward the general. If there is indeed such a thrust, it ought to appear in the temporal structure of the poem as a drive toward conclusiveness, toward placing a final limit on variety and multiplicity. In the final two chapters, therefore, I shall put aside my thematic organization for an analysis of the closing tales, particularly the Canon's Yeoman's Tale and the Parson's Tale; and in the present chapter I shall take up the specific structural issue of the extent of the poem.

Simply stated, the problem is this. In the General Prologue, the Host proposes that each pilgrim should tell two tales on the way to Canterbury and two more on the way home. The pilgrims approve this. However, in the poem as we have it, (a) though there are several clear references to the movement toward Canterbury, there are none to movement homeward (and no indication of arrival at Canterbury); (b) the only pilgrim who actually tells two tales is Chaucer, and he does so only because the Host interrupts and rejects his first attempt; (c) we have no tale at all from any of the five guildsmen, from the Knight's Yeoman, or from the Plowman. Furthermore, when the Host asks the Parson for a tale, he claims that his "ordinaunce" is "almoost fulfild," "for every man, save thou,

hath toold his tale" (125). Since the poem is evidently unfinished, we need not worry over the seven pilgrims from
whom we have no tale; but the reduction of the Host's plan
from four tales apiece to one tale apiece—from many to
one—is quite problematical. Its many ramifications are my
present subject.

The first point I wish to establish is that the evidence that
the Host's original plan is reduced comes very much earlier
than the Parson's Prologue. I am not simply thinking of the
Host's words to the Franklin ("ech of yow moot tellen atte
leste / A tale or two, or breken his biheste" [F698]) and to the
Canon's Yeoman ("Can he [i.e., the Canon] oght telle a myrie
tale or tweye?" [G597]), words commonly cited along with
those to the Parson in discussions of the reduction of the
Host's plan.[1] There is a good deal more evidence than this: we
should suspect even before the General Prologue ends that
there will be only one tale apiece; we should be sure of that
when we have read the Knight's Tale; and our certainty
receives almost constant corroboration.[2]

When the cut falls to the Knight, we are told, "And telle he
moste *his tale,* as was resoun, / By forward and by com-
posicioun" (A848), and again, "he bigan with right a myrie
cheere / *His tale* anon" (A858). The singulars are striking; of
course they may mean only "the tale which this cut obliged
him to tell," not necessarily "his only tale"; but were he to tell
more than one tale, "a tale" in the first instance and "this tale"
in the second would be more appropriate phrases, if not the
even more explicit "his first tale." Then comes a rubric, again
singular and definite: "Heere bigynneth the Knyghtes tale."[3]
Again, a few lines into his tale, the Knight passes quickly over
certain material because

> The remenant of the tale is long ynough.
> I wol nat letten eek noon of this route;
> Lat every felawe telle his tale aboute,
> And lat se now who shal the soper wynne.   (A891)

110

This time the singular is definitive: the rubric is not primary evidence, the two singular phrases in the General Prologue are perhaps ambiguous; but this singular can only mean that the Knight regards the "forward" as requiring a single tale from every member of the fellowship. Since it may be taken as granting its definitiveness retrospectively to the earlier singulars, we may safely say that within the space of forty lines we are told four times that the scope of the poem will be confined to one tale per pilgrim. Furthermore, the Knight implies here that if he does not impose some economy on his telling he may hinder someone else. This suggests an important limitation on the scope of the whole; there is time, or space, for twenty-nine tales only if each teller observes a certain moderation. This is a major modification of the sense of scope implied by the Host's original spacious proposal.[4]

After the tale we find a further series of singular phrases: another rubric, "Heere is ended the Knyghtes tale"; "Whan that the Knyght had thus his tale ytoold" (A3109); "the Knyghtes tale" (A3119 and 3127); the Miller's "my tale" (A3157); "But told his cherles tale in his manere" (A3169); and another rubric, "Heere bigynneth the Millere his tale."

Moreover, a deeper consideration should have emerged in the mind of the attentive reader at this point. He should feel not only from the rubrics and other casual references but from the tale itself that he has read, not "a tale by the Knight," but "the Knight's tale." The definite article is appropriate because the tale is definitive. It defines the Knight. It suits him so richly that any further full utterance from him would be anticlimactic and diffusive, or else merely repetitious. It therefore presumptively also defines what will be meant by "tale" in general: a characterizing utterance, implying a world view; it causes us to look from now on for a fitness between tale and teller, to think of tale and teller as an unassailable unit, whose oneness would collapse if the teller told another tale. This is an effect to which the length, finish, and sublimity of the Knight's Tale contribute. Had one of the lesser tales, say the Physician's Tale, been the first, we might legitimately have expected a free and open-ended potpourri; but since we must feel instead that the Knight has pressed himself to the limit of both philosophy and art in this performance, he has "namoore to telle." No further definition of him through storytelling is conceivable.[5]

Furthermore, in contemplating this definitiveness, we are forced to recollect the portrait in the General Prologue, whereby several further considerations of singularity emerge. There is only one knight, as there is only one representative of each other class. Should not a similar representativeness operate in the tales, that is, should not each representative pilgrim be himself adequately represented by a single tale? Furthermore, each individual portrait is unified, composed of a reasonably simple set of coherent details; this simplicity and coherence can be reproduced in a one-tale scheme, but hardly in a multi-tale scheme. The General Prologue is also moderate and balanced. This should foreshadow similar qualities among the tales, as well as a balanced relationship between the General Prologue and the body of tales: one tale per pilgrim will create that balance, four will upset it surely. Finally, we may recollect that in the General Prologue the author has felt free to shorten his original proposal: we have not been told "al the condicioun / Of ech of hem"; he has told us of the Nuns' Priest and the Second Nun only "whiche they weren,"[6] and has not differentiated the condition of each of the guildsmen. This selectiveness may prepare us for some similar selectiveness in reporting tales: there may be even fewer than one per pilgrim.

In short, whatever the explanation for the Host's scheme, it is clear by the time of the Miller's Tale that we can expect the poem to encompass no more than one tale per pilgrim. This expectation is amply ratified. First, there is further negative evidence: not only does no one but Chaucer tell two tales, no one, neither Host nor pilgrim, ever speaks of a "first tale"[7] (a few who speak of "tales" will be dealt with shortly). Meanwhile, the singular references are so numerous that only a few need be cited. Chaucer says that the Miller and Reeve were churls, "and harlotrie they tolden bothe two" (A3184). If this statement, that both told "harlotrie," refers to what we actually have, two tales, it implies an early authorial intention of assigning only one tale to a pilgrim. If Chaucer was still intending four apiece when he wrote it, it commits him to writing six more fabliaux, six more tales of "harlotrie," for these characters, which is unlikely. The Reeve ends his tale with the line "Thus have I quyt the Millere in my tale" (A4324); though the phrase "my tale" *before* a tale may mean "the tale (among my several) that I am about to tell," at the end of a tale it is not likely to mean "the tale (among my several) that I have just told" (for that one would say "this tale"), but rather "the one tale which is my contribution to our game." The Shipman, Summoner, and Franklin all use the same phrase, "my tale," and so does Chaucer after the Host stops *Sir Thopas* but before he invites him to try something else (B2117). The Host thanks the Nuns' Priest for "youre tale" (B4650). The Host blesses three tellers, the Shipman (B1626), the Nuns' Priest (B4638, 4650), and the Physician (C304), in a formal and valedictory way that would be inappropriate if they were to hold forth again; and the Franklin utters a similar blessing to the Squire (F680). The rubrics continue to be definitive, though four—"the Monkes tale De Casibus," "the Nonnes Preestes tale of the Cok and Hen, Chauntecleer and Pertelote," "the Marchantes tale of Januarie," (cf. also "Thus endeth here my tale of Januarie" [E2417]), and "the Maunciples tale of the Crowe"—are exceptions.

The Host's invitations continue to suggest that the "forward" can be fulfilled with a single tale. To the Man of Law he says, "Telle us a tale anon, as forward is" (B34), and continues,

> Acquiteth yow now of youre biheeste;
> Thanne have ye do youre devoir atte leeste.   (B38)

Though "atte leeste" seems to leave open the possibility of a

further tale or tales, it is clear that one will do; and this is
reinforced by the Man of Law's reply:

> "Hooste," quod he, "*depardieux*, ich assente;
> To breke forward is nat myn entente.
> Biheste is dette, and I wole holde fayn
> Al my biheste." (B42)

And his claim to know no tale that Chaucer has not told
already, his consequent bafflement, "But of my tale how shal
I doon this day?" (B90),[8] and his decision to speak in prose
(even though he does not) make little sense if he still has to
come up with three more. The same can be said of Chaucer's
claim that "oother tale certes kan I noon" (B1898) than *Sir
Thopas* (even if he too turns out to know another).

After the Man of Law's Tale the Host invites the Parson in
similar words: "Telle us a tale, as was thi forward yore"
(B1167). His phrase to Chaucer, "syn oother folk han sayd"
(B1895), implies that they have fulfilled their agreement. To
the Monk he says, "For ye shul telle a tale trewely" (B3115);
this is an absolute statement, i.e., unqualified by any "now" or
"next" to suggest that he means only "it is your turn now," and
not "you have obliged yourself in general to tell a tale." His
invitation to the Clerk,

> Telle us som myrie tale, by youre fey!
> For what man that is entred in a pley,
> He nedes moot unto the pley assente, (E11)

suggests that the "pley" requires "som . . . tale," though he
may only mean that the Clerk must tell a tale now since he has
asked him to. His request to the Squire is inconclusive in itself
("com neer, if it your wille be, / And sey somwhat of love"
[F2]), but the Squire's reply gives it significance:

> I wol seye as I kan
> With hertly wyl; for I wol nat rebelle
> Agayn youre lust; a tale wol I telle. (F6)

114

Since the Host has said, "if it youre wille be," the Squire's resolution not to rebel is best taken with reference to the general "forward," not to the specific request that he take a turn now; it follows that the Squire regards "a tale" as fulfilling his agreement. The Franklin agrees after the tale that the Squire has met his obligation: "In feith, Squier, thow hast thee wel yquit" (F673).

Then comes the Host's unequivocal statement to the Franklin:

wel thou woost
That ech of yow moot tellen atte leste
A tale or two, or breken his biheste,   (F698)

and his use of the same phrase to the Canon's Yeoman:

Can he oght telle a myrie tale or tweye,
With which he glade may this compaignye?   (G598)

This is strictly speaking irrelevant, since the Canon was not a party to the original agreement, but the suggestion is that "a tale or tweye" will entitle the Canon to full membership in the fellowship. Finally we have the equally unequivocal statement to the Parson that one tale suffices:

"Lordynges everichoon,
Now lakketh us no tales mo than oon.
Fulfilled is my sentence and my decree;
I trowe that we han herd of ech degree;
Almoost fulfild is al myn ordinaunce.
I pray to God, so yeve hym right good chaunce,
That telleth this tale to us lustily.
Sire preest," quod he, "artow a vicary?
Or artow a person? sey sooth, by thy fey!
Be what thou be, ne breke thou nat oure pley;
For every man, save thou, hath toold his tale."   (I25)

All of these passages are consistent with the supposition

that the understood agreement is for "a tale or two" each, with a certain expectation that few if any pilgrims will actually tell two tales, "one or two" being simply a conventional or softened way, consistent with the generally informal style and atmosphere of the poem, of saying "one."[9] Though the tale-telling is a "game," it also, by virtue of the "forward," takes on the aspect of a duty, a "devoir," and with that comes the common human impulse to content oneself with the minimal fulfillment of duty, to do one's "devoir atte leeste." "One or two" allows the Host freedom to interrupt Chaucer and suggest he tell another tale; it allows the Monk, with sudden eagerness, to propose "the lyf of Seint Edward" (B3160) as well as "tragedies," but it also allows the Knight to stop the tragedies, the Host to urge the Monk then to tell something else, and, conversely, the Monk to regret his eagerness and "lat another telle, as I have toold" (B3997). It allows the Friar to promise "of a somonour swich a tale or two," and the Summoner to top this by promising "tales two or thre / Of freres" (D842, 847)—just as it allows both to content themselves in fact with just one tale (unless the Summoner regards the anecdote in his prologue as a tale).[10]

We have, then, massive evidence of all sorts to assure the attentive reader early that he can expect the poem to end after about thirty tales, and constant reinforcement of this expectation all through. I wish to stress that the evidence is both massive and early. To many readers, I may well appear to be laboring the obvious, since virtually everyone grants that the plan changed at some point. But it still seems worth marshalling all the evidence, large and small, especially since it does not seem to be generally granted that there is so much to bring forward beyond the Host's words to the Franklin and the Parson. It seems to me also important that there is so much evidence so early: the reader is subtly encouraged almost from the start to expect the whole to encompass about thirty tales. There are, however, several forces which oppose or weaken that expectation. There must be, first of all, some lingering memory of the original proposal, never explicitly abjured; there is also the ambiguity of the phrase "one or two." Furthermore, we never quite know what will happen next: if we know by the time of the Miller's Tale that the norm will be one tale apiece, we also know that there will be no settled order of tellers, and that a tale told by one pilgrim may suddenly generate another tale from another pilgrim. The Host is quite willing to accept these sudden volunteers; the poem seems to proceed by a process of open-ended addition, especially since there are so many pilgrims that the average reader finds himself unable or disinclined to keep in mind just who has "told" and who remains. And the very right to select on the part of the narrator, which I have listed earlier as a possible limiting factor, can also serve to increase uncertainty: right up to the Parson's Prologue, even someone who has kept count has the right to expect more. Furthermore, if there are "early" indications that limit our expectations, there are two "late" surprises that open the possibility of further expansion. These are the addition to the company of the Canon's Yeoman, and the departure the Host makes from what has amounted to his regular practice of only offering one turn each when he asks a tale of the Cook at Bobbe-up-and-doun, even though the Cook has in fact told a tale much earlier.[11]

What we have, in short, to borrow the terms of Barbara Herrnstein Smith's *Poetic Closure*,[12] is a dynamic of continuation and closure. The poem begins (like spring) by generating a series of forces for continuation: the opening sentence generates the next several; these generate the descriptions of the pilgrims and finally the Host's plan; this in turn generates the tales and also the links; the links maintain the drive toward continuation by prompting individual tales in a seemingly random way; and certain tales also cause other tales. A further force for continuation is the voice of the eager poet, with his humble insistence that he must "reherce as ny as evere he kan / Everich a word," and his promise to tell "al the remenant of oure pilgrimage" (A733, 724). But working ever against these expansive and additive forces are other forces that make for closure, and in particular what might be called a "pattern of diminishment." This appears in various ways within the General Prologue. The first hint of it is in the first group of pilgrims described, wherein the Squire's portrait is shorter than the Knight's, and the Yeoman's shorter than the Squire's. The second group, also of three—Prioress, Nun, and Priest—is reduced to only one portrait. The same lessening occurs in the group Parson-Plowman. The five guildsmen receive a single composite portrait, and Chaucer gets none at all. For twenty-nine pilgrims we have twenty-two portraits; we have not, as I have said, been told "al the condicioun / Of ech of hem," nor have we been told "al the condicioun" even of the twenty-two described, since in three cases (Cook, Parson, and Manciple) we are told nothing of "array." There is also the implicit diminishment of each professional class to a single representative (which surely lies behind the failure to describe the Priest, the Second Nun, and the individual city artisans, of whom four are in the textile trades, the fifth a carpenter like the Reeve).[13] Set against this pattern of diminishment is a weaker pattern of addition: a portrait of the Host is added.

The pattern might also be thought of as an increasing selectivity or generality, as if once we get the idea Chaucer need not spell out all the particulars. I think that is exactly what happens with the tales. Realizing—early, in my opinion—that the professional scheme of the poem, the idea of hearing from "ech degree," was amply carried out even before each pilgrim had told one tale, Chaucer reduced its scope. And so the pattern continues. The Host's "two tales each way" diminishes, in his own words, from "one or two" or "one at least" to "one," and in fact to one. Seven pilgrims not only tell no tales but are never mentioned further. There are additions, but the very additions are themselves diminished: two more prospective pilgrims arrive, the Canon and his Yeoman, but only one stays to tell a tale; Chaucer's second tale depends on the foreshortening of his first; the Monk proposes to tell the life of Saint Edward, but never does so; the Cook's second tale is excused. The Monk's Tale is diminished in length by the Knight. Even Chaucer's failure to complete the Cook's and Squire's tales may be a function of this pattern.[14]

There is a further diminishment in the scope of the reported journey: we go from expecting a report of the journey in both directions, to expecting a report of the journey to Canterbury only, to finally realizing that we have not even been brought quite to Canterbury. This is another reduction to oneness, and a further development of the poet's selectiveness. As against the Host's original plan, which is "slack," merely filling up a certain predetermined time, and involving the anticlimax of the return trip, the poet imposes further closure and meaning by introducing a clear movement toward a goal. Furthermore, that goal is the "authoritative," chosen goal of the shrine and its spiritual meanings rather than the "experiential," necessary goal of the Tabard or home. It is not clear at what point we realize that the reported movement will be in one direction only; perhaps we realize it at the same time that we realize we shall hear at most one complete tale per pilgrim. That is especially likely if the latter realization is combined with a response to the Knight's and the Host's sense of urgency: our original expansive and leisurely sense of time has been diminished.[15] In any case we do realize by the time of the Parson's Prologue that we shall have no homeward journey, and at the very end we realize that the poem has not taken us even to Canterbury; and we realize also that a one-way journey accords completely with teleological expectations otherwise engendered—as for example in the opening sentences, which speak only of going to Canterbury, not home from it.[16]

One might do well to think of the poem in terms of "becoming." The pilgrims are becoming pilgrims; the poem is a process which works mysteriously toward its goal. I feel this if I compare the artificial sense of community at the beginning to the fuller, more realized version in the Parson's Prologue. The poem works the way the *Consolation of Philosophy* works: the goal appears only gradually. Philoso-

119

phy shows Boethius that his true home is with God: "that is the contre that thou requerist," to which "thow . . . shalt mowen retourne hool and sownd" (Book 4, meter 1, prose 1). So too in the *Canterbury Tales*, by the end the literal return home is obsolete, though it is right that it should have been contemplated at the beginning. A similar effect takes place in the ninth book of Saint Augustine's *Confessions*, when Monica dies at Ostia, where she has been waiting to take ship back home to Africa. Augustine makes much of the difference between that false homecoming she contemplated and the true homecoming that her death occasions. Boethius associates the notion of a goal with the One as against the many. "Eyther alle thinges ben referrid and brought to noght, and floteren withouten governour, despoyled of oon as of hire propre heved; or elles, yif ther be any thing to which that alle thinges tenden and hyen to, that thing muste ben the sovereyn good of alle goodes. . . . That good is the fyn of alle thinges" (Book 3, prose 11). The poem may also be related to what Boethius says on the relation of fate to Providence. The pilgrimage goes as it were by fate, by motion through particular time; but Providence takes over at the end.

Let me insist again that this pattern of diminishment, with the expectations of firm and imminent closure that it engenders, is not absolute, but always exists in a dynamic interplay with various "open" or "expansive" or "additive" tendencies, with forces that make us expect continuation. We never expect closure with certainty until the poem actually ends. As Smith insists, throughout our reading of the poem we merely "test" structural principles; it is not until the end that the total pattern is revealed. Throughout we are caught up in "experience," and in tentative definitions of it; finally the poem itself imposes its authority on us. Nevertheless, I think I have shown that the very structure of the poem contains a tension between variety and particularity on the one hand, the impulse to tell more and more stories, and unity, limitation, generic definition on the other, the impulse to confine the poem to a manageable structure and impose on it a goal which is, at least in retrospect, definitive. In the next two chapters my purpose is to show how the concluding parts of the poem embody a thematic confirmation of those structural elements which generate closure.

Appendix to Chapter Five
Does the Cook Expect to
Tell a Second Tale?

The Cook seems to expect to have a later chance to tell a tale
when he replies to the Host's insults as follows:

> "'Sooth pley, quaad pley,' as the Flemyng seith.
> And therfore, Herry Bailly, by thy feith,
> Be thou nat wrooth, er we departen heer,
> Though that my tale be of an hostileer.
> But nathelees I wol nat telle it yit;
> But er we parte, ywis, thou shalt be quit."
> And therwithal he lough and made cheere,
> And seyde his tale, as ye shul after heere.   (A4364)

The phrases "er we departen heer" and "er we parte" seem
even to allude to the end of the return journey. On the other
hand, he says "my tale," and the narrator says "his tale."
Furthermore, the consideration that prompts the Cook to
offer his tale, "God forbede that we stynte heere" (A4339), in
conjunction with the lines that precede it, implies that his tale
will deal with "herberwynge" and be motivated by professional animosity (he is pleased to see a miller fooled; cooks
depend on millers). Perhaps it is this specific implication,
rather than the normal professional animosity between cooks
and innkeepers (i.e., hostlers, hosts) that causes the Host's
insults. And the tale does introduce the room-and-board
business: Perkyn is "of a craft of vitailliers" (A4366) like the

Host, who "served us with vitaille atte beste"(A749), and he moves in with a whore, who keeps a shop, presumably a food shop such as that Perkyn worked in previously. All this suggests that the present Cook's Tale may well be the one to be told "of an hostileer" (for the application of "of" to a subordinate character, cf. the Nuns' Priest's reference to "this widwe, of which I telle yow my tale" [B4014]; contrast the Man of Law's "Of Custance is my tale *specially*" [B1125] and the Wife's "This knyght, of which my tale is *specially*" [D983]). "I wol nat telle it yit" may then simply mean that the hostler does not appear at the beginning of the tale (unless "hostileer" is an ironic term for the whore, which I doubt); "er we departen heer" and "er we parte" may refer either to the present subject (cf. "God forbede that we stynte heere") or to the fact that the Cook has ridden up next to the Host, the regular teller's position (cf. B1888-89, 3117, 4000; F1; H12).

In this light, the Cook's remarks may be paraphrased as follows. "True play is bad play, and therefore, since my tale is true ("a litel jape that fil in oure citee") and—in part—of a hostler, it is likely to seem a bad jest to you, Herry Bailly, and so to make you angry before I leave your side (or, before we leave this subject of "herberwynge"). But please don't be angry. I'm not going to tell the hostler part right off, but I'll have my chance to insult you back before I finish my tale." (The purpose of specifying this last would be that he feels he ought to trade insults immediately with the Host; that's the ordinary expectation, and since that doesn't fit in with the tale, he at least has to predict the moment when he will get to it.) Or "I wol nat telle it yit" means, "I won't reveal right now how the hostler fits in; I won't spoil my story by making my insults in advance."

6. Experience and Authority II: The Canon's Yeoman's Tale

Group G offers a reprise of conflict between authority and experience. The Second Nun's Tale is altogether authoritative: told by a religious, about a saint (and a bossy one), who is presented as a model of Christian action and who regards marriage as anything but an arena for the free play of experience. It regards ordinary physical experience as "dremes" (G262) or "prison" (G71); Cecilia rejects physical experience for virginity, an integral life of unity with God and membership in the community of Christians. Valerian, Tiburce, and Maximus and his soldiers are first integrated from the physical world of the pagans (whose many gods are "stoon" [G500]) into the Christian community where oneness reigns ("O Lord, o feith, o God, withouten mo, / O cristendom" [G208]), then transmuted to the "bettre lif . . . / That nevere shal be lost"(G324). The world of experience, or at least the voice of common sense, makes brief appearances in Valerian's expectations on the first night of marriage and in his suspicion that Cecilia's angel lover is another man, and in Tiburce's remark that the savor of roses and lilies he detects when he enters Cecilia's house is odd for "this tyme of the yeer" (G246). But both are quickly enough "chaunged... al in another kynde" (G252); it is a tale in which alchemy works.[1]

The Canon's Yeoman's Tale, on the other hand, rivals the Wife of Bath's Prologue in the rein it gives to experience; indeed, it is freer than that prologue of ironic instrusions of authority. Its experiential nature is emphasized by its context: the suddenly appearing Canon and his Yeoman are outside the "authoritative" structure of both fellowship and pilgrimage; they challenge the definition of the fellowship by testing whether it can open itself to admit them. They are also, as characters, outside the defining (and confining) influence of the General Prologue. The Yeoman as teller has no prior portrait weighing on him; and if his tale in large part offers us an extended portrait of the Canon, that portrait still differs from those in the General Prologue in being provided not by the author but by a character.

Chaucer gives, to be sure, a brief portrait of his own at the start, but unlike those in the General Prologue it cannot get beyond the externals of clothing and sweat, and a guess from the clothing at profession:

> At Boghtoun under Blee us gan atake
> A man that clothed was in clothes blake,
> And under that he hadde a whyt surplys.
> His hakeney, that was al pomely grys,
> So swatte that it wonder was to see;
> It semed he had priked miles three.
> The hors eek that his yeman rood upon
> So swatte that unnethe myghte he gon.
> Aboute the peytrel stood the foom ful hye;
> He was of foom al flekked as a pye.
> A male tweyfoold on his croper lay.
> It semed that he caried lite array.
> Al light for somer rood this worthy man,
> And in myn herte wondren I bigan
> What that he was, til that I understood
> How that his cloke was sowed to his hood;
> For which, whan I longe hadde avysed me,
> I demed hym som chanoun for to be.
> His hat heeng at his bak doun by a laas,
> For he hadde riden moore than trot or paas;
> He hadde ay priked lik as he were wood.

> A clote-leef he hadde under his hood
> For swoot, and for to keep his heed from heete.
> But it was joye for to seen hym swete!
> His forheed dropped as a stillatorie,
> Were ful of plantayne and of paritorie. (G581)

Chaucer notes the sweat again and again, as if it were the one fact he can fasten on; we may note that it is a useful symbol for experience. This tentative portrait pales, however, before the full account the Yeoman eventually gives. The relation of portrait to narrative, in the fabliaux and in the poem as a whole, is regularly a paradigm for the relation of authority to experience, but ordinarily they end up balanced: though the narrative is more detailed, it is discernibly "contained" in the portrait, as authority contains and predicts most experience. Here we have a similar relation, but one in which there is no balance. The experience is far richer, far more accurate, a surprise. The author makes a standard association of clothing and profession: by the "authority" of the hood he rightly guesses that the newcomer is a canon. But, though he falls by accident, or by a standard association of canons with alchemy, into an alchemical simile ("His forheed dropped as a stillatorie"), he is not equipped as the Yeoman is, from his experience, to describe the Canon with full accuracy through narrative.

The Host's questions (G597ff.) gradually draw out the full truth. These questions are based on "authority," stereotyped expectations. "Telle what he is," i.e., name his profession (and we shall know him). Is he a clerk (since he has a threadbare cloak)? How can he be both reverend and "sluttish"? Where does he come from? The Yeoman, still experientially disposed, never does name a profession or a provenance, which may invite generalization, but continues to reveal particulars. These associate both the Canon and himself with multiplicity, with experiment, and with failure:

> "Peter!" quod he, "God yeve it harde grace,

127

> I am so used in the fyr to blowe
> That it hath chaunged my colour, I trowe.
> I am nat wont in no mirour to prie,
> But swynke soore and lerne multiplie.
> We blondren evere and pouren in the fir,
> And for al that we faille of oure desir,
> For evere we lakken oure conclusioun. (G672)

The Canon then attempts to stop him, the Host insists that he "telle on," the Canon rides away, and the Yeoman proceeds without further prompting from the Host. His "tale" is in two parts. *Prima pars* is a somewhat disordered account of alchemy and of his own experience as an apprentice alchemist, leading to a climactic account of a particular failed experiment (what I shall call "the explosion scene"); *pars secunda*, or the tale proper, is a story of how a canon alchemist, not the Yeoman's Canon, duped a priest; it leads the Yeoman to a final abjuration of the art.

Perhaps the most obvious way in which the Canon's Yeoman's Tale explores the relation of one to many lies in its thus presenting us with two canon-alchemists: one the Yeoman's Canon who appears, then rides away; the other, whom I shall call the "second canon," who dupes the priest in the Yeoman's *pars secunda*. According to the poem's standard mode of generalizing, we might expect that, despite the Yeoman's insistence that the second canon is not his Canon, the two will share professional characteristics in such a way as to be indistinguishable from each other, and together provide a composite portrait of the typical canon-alchemist.

To some extent this is what happens. The Yeoman promises an exposition of the art:

> Now wolde God my wit myghte suffise
> To tellen al that longeth to that art! (G716)

We will learn the secrets of the art of alchemy, as we have learned the secrets of pardoning, of summoning, of begging

Experience and Authority II: The Canon's Yeoman's Tale

(in the Summoner's Tale), or milling, of weather forecasting
(from Nicholas), of wifery. And we are told certain external
signs of how to recognize an alchemist:

> And everemoore, where that evere they goon,
> Men may hem knowe by smel of brymstoon.
> ....
> Lo thus by smellyng and threedbare array,
> If that men liste, this folk they knowe may.
> And if a man wol aske hem pryvely
> Why they been clothed so unthriftily,
> They right anon wol rownen in his ere,
> And seyn if that they espied were,
> Men wolde hem slee by cause of hir science.   (G885, 896)

The first Canon has already lived up to these generalizations:
Chaucer and the Host have noticed his "lite array," the
Yeoman has seemed reluctant to give an open, truthful answer to the Host's question about it; the Canon has obviously
feared "espial." Though it is not said that he smells, his smell
may explain why he has kept apart while the Yeoman talked
(cf. G685). The second canon shares these signs also: the smell
(he "wolde infecte al a toun" [G973]), the apparent poverty
(he needs a loan from the priest), the fear of death if his craft
is exposed:

> For, and men knewen al my soutiltee,
> By God, they wolden han so greet envye
> To me, by cause of my philosophye,
> I sholde be deed.   (G1374)

Further, both victimize others, and the Yeoman hints that
both are in league with the devil (G916ff., 984, 1069ff.; cf. also
the smell of brimstone).

Thus far, then, the appearance of the pair on the pilgrimage, and the utterances of the Yeoman, though they
extend the "many" by introducing us to one more deceitful

129

profession, seem to reinforce the "one" by amalgamating the practitioners of this profession into a single type, and also by amalgamating the profession itself into the general class "deceitful professions." And though the Canon stays mum, the Yeoman also reinforces our sense that the practitioners of deceit feel a compulsion to reveal their secrets. But thus far only. For side by side with this generalizing impulse lies an impulse to single out and make distinctions. We see this impulse in the Yeoman's distinction between his canon and the second canon (though of course he brings the need to make it on himself by making them sound so similar). We can see it somewhat more importantly in his separating shrewish canons from "worshipful chanons religious" (G992). But we see it most of all in certain sharp distinctions which we ourselves must make between the two canons, and between the first canon and his Yeoman's estimate of him. The Yeoman's own distinction has given us the direction of the first set of distinctions; the second set we clearly must make altogether on our own.

The distinction between the two canons, though many critics refuse to accept it,[2] is very clear and very important. The second canon is a typical confidence man, an out-and-out cheat. Though he has had to familiarize himself with alchemical terms, apparatus, and procedures, the tale give no indication that he actually practices alchemy. He practices only on his victims; his only aim is to enrich himself by cheating others. Though the first Canon also wants to enrich himself, he focuses his hope not on a confidence game but on experiment. To be sure, he attracts others to his work because he needs their money, and to that extent victimizes them; but they become his associates rather than his victims. I do not wish to whitewash the first Canon; clearly he and his Yeoman ride up to the pilgrims with some hope of duping them ("ye wolde nat forgoon his aqueyntaunce / For muchel good" [G611]); and the Yeoman also admits that "To muchel folk we doon illusioun" (G673). But there are central distinctions in the manner of illusion. The second canon sells his "receite" for forty pounds and disappears. He is never seen again by the priest; no one knows where he lives: "he is here and there; / He is so variaunt, he abit nowhere" (G1175). The first Canon's method is to "borwe gold" and attempt to multiply it, to "make hem wenen, at the leeste weye, / That of a pound we koude make tweye" (G677). That is false, and yet "ay we han good hope / It for to doon, and after it we grope" (G679). The second canon has no hope himself, he merely capitalizes on the hope of others; and he does not "grope" himself, he cynically urges the priest to "grope" (G1236; see also 1154-55, 1329). The first Canon's method seems to be to gather accomplices along with their capital; the Yeoman is one, and the several fellow experimenters in the explosion scene seem to be others. Though his dwelling is shady, "In the suburbes of a toun . . . / Lurkynge in hernes and in lanes blynde" (G658), it is not "nowhere." He is no less a victim of illusion than his "victims." Whereas the Yeoman seethes with anger at the second canon (e.g. at G1299ff.), the anger he feels at his own experience he directs at himself or the art rather than at his master; he accuses his master only of "bringing him first into that game" (G708). If it is a confidence game, it is so infinitely more elaborate, long-term, committed, and communal an enterprise, so much closer to the wellsprings of hope and trust, so much more "ernest" than "game," as to constitute in any case an utter contrast to the second canon's simple bilking of the priest, the brief work of a few hours.[3]

Indeed, the Yeoman makes his Canon even more attractive than he apparently intends to. The Canon belongs with the Pardoner and the Wife of Bath as a third major representative of experience. If he is less willing than either to redeem himself by confessing his secrets, he is also less cynical than the Pardoner: the Pardoner's counterpart in cynicism is the second canon. The Canon seems rather to have undergone a growth similar to the Wife's. She starts out regarding marriage as an arena for making victims out of her husbands, but gradually becomes herself the victim; or, alternatively, she gradually finds marriage an arena for broader and more complex personal experience, for a deep labyrinth of suffering and hope. Alchemy for the Canon is a similarly complex arena for both victimizing and being victimized, and for both suffering and hope.

The Canon's commitment to experience takes the form of experiment. His experimentation is anti-authoritative in every way. It looks to the future, not the past. It is individual: he hopes to do what no one else has done. It embraces variety, in materials, in constant adjustment of the experiment, and in the aim of multiplying: it makes the arrogant assumption that one can be many, that gold takes the surface form of other metals. There is, of course, an implicit striving for unity, for the single "elixir" which underlies various metals. As Bruce Rosenberg has shown, the experiment involved "a conjunction of opposites: male and female, fire and water, sun and moon, spirit and body."[4] The alchemist attempts a form of marriage. But since the goal is evanescent, the experiments remain mired in multiplicity. Or one might state the Canon's problem this way: the unity he wants is the elixir, the multiplicity he wants is the multiplication of money; what he has instead is an intractable variety of materials—listed in effective disorder by the Yeoman—while his money dwindles into nothingness. His experiments presume to question the "authority" of matter itself, and perhaps implicitly the authority of God the creator, and Theseus's "cheyne of love," of things bound "in certeyn boundes that they may nat flee" (A2993).[5] In all these ways he is a serious exponent of the experiential mode, to my mind the most serious in the poem. (He may also, of course, since Chaucerian irony has many levels, be seen as the most fanatic of all the male intellectuals in the poem. But that side of him lurks in the corners of the poem; it is not a major element.)

The clash between experience and authority is dramatized by the Yeoman's conversion. The Canon rides off to continue "lurkynge in hernes"; the Yeoman returns to the center, joins the community of ordinary men, and enters it fully by confessing. The release he feels is that of a man who has been enslaved by the tyranny of a misdirected will, lost among the meaningless data of a world without authoritative organization and guidance, now fixed by returning to a public order. His seven years' experience of alchemy, which has, instead of transforming lead into gold, only transformed his ruddy face into "leden hewe," have brought him to the general conclusion that alchemy is a failure:

> Noght helpeth us, oure labour is in veyn.
> Ne eek oure spirites ascencioun,
> Ne oure materes that lyen al fix adoun,
> Mowe in oure werkyng no thyng us availle,
> For lost is al oure labour and travaille;
> And al the cost, a twenty devel waye,
> Is lost also, which we upon it laye.   (G783)

He has himself become an authority, a living exemplum: "Lat every man be war by me for evere!" (G737). He is fond of proverbs ("al thyng which that shineth as the gold / Nis nat gold" [G963]) and sententious remarks that go beyond alchemy:

> For unto shrewes joye it is and ese
> To have hir felawes in peyne and disese.
> Thus was I ones lerned of a clerk.   (G748)

He ends his tale by quoting the alchemical authorities, who themselves cite the authority of God: to Christ, the philosophers' stone is "so lief and deere / That he wol nat that it discovered be" (G1468). This is an authoritative reservation of experience by God. The Yeoman concludes (unlike the Canon, who cannot "reach conclusion") by acknowledging ignorance and accepting limits on human experience:

> Thanne conclude I thus, sith that God of hevene
> Ne wil nat that the philosophres nevene
> How that a man shal come unto this stoon,

133

> I rede, as for the beste, lete it goon.
> For whoso maketh God his adversarie,
> As for to werken any thyng in contrarie
> Of his wil, certes, never shal he thryve.   (G1478)[6]

As Theseus said, the contrary of this is willfulness. One is reminded of the Yeoman's curse on the future tense:

> That futur temps hath maad men to dissevere,
> In trust therof, from al that evere they hadde.   (G876)

The Canon's special devotion to willfulness, to his own will as against God's, lies in his compulsive use of the future tense; we leave him saying, "the nexte tyme I wol fonde" (G951).

If the Yeoman's integration into the company marks his acceptance of its implicit authority, the Canon's riding off marks his aloneness, his particularity: he is separated not only from the large company but even from his single accomplice. We must see him, however, not merely as avoiding exposure. He rides off because there is no possibility of being understood here in this centric, representative, perhaps even pious group. For despite the Yeoman's contempt there shines through his account an image of the Canon as an honest, dedicated searcher who will not be defeated. Chaucer is strongly interested, there is no doubt, in the Yeoman's conversion: the tale upholds the superiority of the way of authority over the way of experience; but he also grants the way of experience its full value.

We are made to feel this value in several ways. First, we feel it through the Yeoman's passion: the very vehemence with which he cries out against alchemy suggests how strong an attraction it has had for him. It seems, in fact, to attract him still. His lists of materials and apparatus are more loving than satirical; nor is he yet sufficiently removed to speak in the third person—he says "we," not "they" he speaks of "oure labour," "oure sleightes," "oure craft," of what "we lost." The Yeoman is very good on the interplay of hope with loss and failure. This subject provides a kind of refrain for him, the deepest outlet for his passion; but it also draws sympathy from us, not only for him but for the Canon who has chosen to remain a loser. Though the Yeoman has finally tired of failure, one feels that paradoxically it is the very failures that, when combined with hope, provide the challenge and ineluctable attraction of alchemy:

> We blondren evere and pouren in the fir,
> And for al that we faille of oure desir,
> For evere we lakken oure conclusioun.
> . . . .
> Yet is it fals, and ay we han good hope
> It for to doon, and after it we grope.
> But that science is so fer us biforn,
> We mowen nat, although we hadden it sworn,
> It overtake, it slit awey so faste.
> It wole us maken beggers atte laste.   (G672, 683)

As he speaks of groping and failure, the Yeoman seems himself to be groping for a way to get hold of his narrative and descriptive material. His shifts back and forth among lists of supplies and equipment, a chronological account of a particular day's experiment, expressions of personal regret and bitterness, explanations of how people are sucked in to contribute money and then to join the quest—all seem to imitate the alchemist's jumbled and groping attempt to transmute his intractable materials.

The refrain of failure continues:

> For alle oure sleightes we kan nat conclude.   (G773)

> For bothe two, by my savacioun,
> Concluden in multiplicacioun
> Ylike wel, whan they han al ydo;
> This is to seyn, they faillen bothe two.   (G851)

They seek the philosophers' stone, which would make them

135

The One and the Many

"siker ynow." But "he wol nat come us to"; this would drive them crazy,

> But that good hope crepeth in oure herte,
> Supposynge evere, though we sore smerte,
> To be releeved by hym afterward.
> Swich supposyng and hope is sharp and hard;
> I warne yow wel, it is to seken evere.
> That futur temps hath maad men to dissevere,
> In trust therof, from al that evere they hadde. (G876)

Among the merits of these moving passages is the fact that their imagery is drawn from quicksilver, which "crepeth" and "slit awey so faste," and whose softness and apparent tractability keeps the alchemist from seeing that his hope is "sharp and hard," that it is the very knife that is causing him to "sore smerte." He blinds himself further from the present reality of failure by speaking constantly in the future tense. One senses that the Yeoman has rarely heard the Canon speak in the present tense, with its grasp on reality, has heard him instead constantly speaking of what will happen, of what they will do. This is a knife, too, which "dissevers" men not only from "all they ever had" but from what they were and are.

The operation of the hard knife of hope is thus an ironic subtraction or division, a diminishment, instead of a multiplication or addition:

> Yet of that art they kan nat wexen sadde,
> For unto hem it is a bitter sweete,—
> So semeth it,—for nadde they but a sheete,
> Which that they myghte wrappe hem in a-nyght,
> And a brat to walken in by daylyght,
> They wolde hem selle and spenden on this craft.
> They kan nat stynte til no thyng be laft. (G883)

Yet surely the diminishment is not ironic in the sense that it is perceptible only to an outsider such as the Yeoman now is. Better to suppose that this naked confrontation of his work is a conscious choice of the Canon's, a kind of *via negativa* through which he hopes to reach his plenteous goal. That is the implication of "bitter sweete"; the biting of the knife is felt, and yet so is the sweetness of hope, and the sweetness of commitment. The phrase makes explicit the ambivalence that not only the alchemist feels but that the Yeoman and we feel toward this slippery science.

There are yet deeper sources of sympathy, however. The Yeoman speaks so often and so feelingly of hope and loss, labor and failure, and commitment in the face of failure, that we are made to reflect on these experiences in general. The passages draw their fullest emotional power from deep human impulses, from the general human experience of loss, of hope in the future despite loss, of the difficulty of bringing any human enterprise to a conclusion. Every reader must bring to them his own particular response to the experience of seeing the future become the past, but no reader can fail to be moved. They also bring to mind several similar moments elsewhere in the poem. The alchemist's blindness to the dead end of his quest is like that of the three rioters in the Pardoner's Tale, or like Arcite's.[7] "That futur temps" is his version of the "purveiaunce" which keeps the Wife of Bath going, but which the Knight has shown to be properly exercised only by God; one might say that the Yeoman, in his relatively venal way, has seen the same futility in independent human attempts to achieve security ("thanne were we siker ynow") as Theseus has come to see. Nor does Chaucer's own experience seem irrelevant: from the Retraction, from the unfinished state of the poem and its diminished relation to its largest conception, and from its thematic development in the direction of authority, as I have outlined it, we may sense that Chaucer too felt that "we faille of oure desir, / For evere we lakken oure conclusioun."

The climax of the Yeoman's account of his Canon is the great explosion scene. Like the Wife in her Prologue, he

The One and the Many

achieves a rhythm of contraction and expansion, moving now "inward" to detailed accounts of "oure craft"—in part a mere list of equipment, in part an orderly account of the process of an experiment—now "outward" to the reflective passages I have just been commenting on. This rhythm reflects the Yeoman's ambivalence; in the "contracted" passages he seems still wrapped up in the particulars of alchemy, in the expansive passages he attempts to assert his freedom from it. And, as the Wife focuses finally on the climactic scene of tearing out the page from Jankyn's book, he finally focuses with full intensity on the last steps of the experimental process, in which the materials themselves, compressed beyond endurance, explode and tear apart the sides of the "pot," leading him to a final expansive passage of reflection and conclusion. The material of his tale and the materials of the experiment match, if they do not symbolize, the process of his conversion, his movement outward from the confinement of his alchemical experience to a full assertion of the new freedom he feels in the company of pilgrims.

More immediately and germanely, the explosion symbolizes the Canon's attempt to surpass authoritative limits, but does so as it were falsely. He does "make a breakthrough," but only into meaningless fragmentation, not into any transcendent new unity. For the multiplication of gold that he seeks, he gets only division, a messy multiplicity of flying fractions of metal:

> somme of hem synken into the ground—
> Thus han we lost by tymes many a pound—
> And somme are scatered al the floor aboute;
> Somme lepe into the roof. (G915)

This multiplicity of matter is matched by that familiar phenomenon, a multiplicity of opinion, echoing the repetition of "somme":

> Somme seyde it was long on the fir makyng;

138

Experience and Authority II: The Canon's Yeoman's Tale

Somme seyde nay, it was on the blowyng,—
Thanne was I fered, for that was myn office.
"Straw!" quod the thridde, "ye been lewed and nyce.
It was nat tempred as it oghte be."
"Nay," quod the fourthe, "stynt and herkne me.
By cause oure fyr was nat maad of beech,
That is the cause, and oother noon, so theech!" (G929)

A true pandemonium, the Yeoman suggests: "Though that
the feend noght in oure sighte hym shewe, / I trowe he with
us be" (G917). Then, however, into this "greet strif," this
double multiplicity of material and opinion, steps the Canon
with a surprisingly calm voice:

"What," quod my lord, "ther is namoore to doone;
Of thise perils I wol be war eftsoone.
I am right siker that the pot was crased.
Be as be may, be ye no thyng amased;
As usage is, lat swepe the floor as swithe;
Plukke up youre hertes, and beeth glad and blithe."
(G937)

There are complex effects here. The Canon's single-minded
devotion seems powerful enough to resist the fragmentation,
as does his generalizing ability to see this instance in the light
of many like it: sweep up, he says, "as usage is." Yet what a
weariness lies in that phrase, suggesting to us not the singleness of habit but rather an infinite multiplicity of past failures.
The Canon may recognize recurrence, but he seems unable
to recognize its implications. This gives him a remarkable
buoyancy, however, which we are forced to admire even as
he utters the fatal future tense: "Of thise perils I wol be war
eftsoone."

Yet we know that such hope as this is "sharp and hard," a
fact that is underlined by the too easy way that this very
"unifying" voice is itself multiplied in being immediately
echoed by one of those who have just now been striving:

139

> though this thyng myshapped have as now,
> Another tyme it may be well ynow.
> Us moste putte oure good in aventure.
> A marchant, pardee, may nat ay endure,
> Trusteth me wel, in his prosperitee.
> Somtyme his good is drowned in the see,
> And somtyme comth it sauf unto the londe.   (G950)

The mercantile metaphor here is particularly fertile in its echo of earlier "experiential" treatments: we have seen not only the anxiety regarding the sea, and the "bargaynes" and the "chevyssaunce," of the pilgrim Merchant in the General Prologue, but the dubious outcome of the ventures and adventures of the merchant in the Shipman's Tale, and also of January's speculation, as articulated by the Merchant, in the "commune market-place" (E1583) of marriage in opposition to authoritative advice.[8] The last two lines of the passage also echo the vicissitude stressed generally in the Knight's Tale, and particularly Saturn's account of the various unlooked-for disasters he provokes, including "the drenchyng in the see so wan" (A2456). The trust the speaker expresses in fortune and in their own efforts augurs ill; it renders them quite as vulnerable to Saturn's destructive power as Arcite has proven to be.

The Canon's reply is of extraordinary importance for the entire *Canterbury Tales*:

> "Pees!" quod my lord, "the nexte tyme I wol fonde
> To bryngen oure craft al in another plite,
> And but I do, sires, lat me han the wite.
> Ther was defaute in somwhat, wel I woot."   (G954)

In general in the poem, "craft" is an authority-word. "Craft" is the common man's "clergye": it implies a set of skills of which a man may become "master," a "master of the art" corresponding to a "Master of Arts." Since the skills as it were preexist for the practitioner, they represent an authoritative

140

standard to which he apprentices himself and which he gradually attains. Further, since "the craft" means the fellowship of skilled practitioners, it has the unifying, generalizing force of a proper authority. And it implies mastery over chance, also: to learn the carpenter's craft, for example, is to ensure that the houses you build will stand. In the General Prologue, such a complex of meaning lies behind not only the actual use of this word ("But of his craft, to rekene wel his tydes" [A401], "But of his craft, fro Berwyk into Ware" [A692]), but the whole concept of identifying pilgrims by profession. The profession, as I have argued, is in each case an authenticating "company."

But what the Canon says here throws doubt on all this. He acknowledges implicitly that his craft, alchemy, has no such transcendent authority; it is, after all, something neutral which depends for its working on the individual practitioner and his attempts (cf. "fonde") to bring it into some effective "plite." This is very much a matter, not of the past, not of preexisting standards, but of "futur temps," of "supposyng and hope": "the nexte time I wol fonde." The result is conditional ("but I do") and again, dependent on the individual practitioner ("lat me han the wite"). Of course the Canon is attempting to salvage the good name of the craft by placing the inadequacy on himself, not it, and on the particular ("ther was defaute in somwhat"), not alchemy in general. But who is master of the craft if he is not? (The Yeoman has served a seven-year apprenticeship under him.) His words, despite this intent, seem rather to ratify the previous speaker's reference to the merchant's "aventure."

This is, of course, the Yeoman's point: alchemy is "craft," i.e., deception, not "a craft." It lacks the authority that other crafts have because it is not authenticated by results ("we concluden everemoore amys" [G957]). Presumably one dimension of the authority the Yeoman finds in the company of pilgrims is precisely the fact that it includes members of genuine crafts: a cook, a miller, the five guildsmen, etc. Not only is the Canon a loner, but his craft is a misfit, too. And yet the doubt here cast on the authority of "craft" through its element of "aventure" may well be extended further. Saturn has extended his misrule to craft as well as merchandising:

> Myn is the ruyne of the hye halles,
> The fallynge of the toures and of the walles
> Upon the mynour or the carpenter.   (A2465)

Mars, Saturn's agent, touches the crafts as well:

> The hunte strangled with the wilde beres;
> . . . .
> The cook yscalded, for al his longe ladel.
> Noght was forgeten by the infortune of Marte:
> The cartere overryden with his carte,
> Under the wheel ful lowe he lay adoun.   (A2018, 2023)

These brief examples of mishap suggest a saturnine principle: the very materials the craftsman seeks to master may master him. The boars strangle the hunter, the cart rides the carter, the broth cooks the cook, carpenter and miner are buried beneath the structures they erect. A similar principle of "proper" retribution inhabits the professional tales: the summoner is summoned to hell; the preacher-friar shares hot air with his brothers; John the carpenter constructs the instruments by which he is cuckolded; Nicholas the rain forecaster cannot foresee his own need for water; Symkyn the miller is out-wrestled. The Pardoner is silenced by the Host's crude riposte, redefining relics, and silenced even more effectively by the kiss through which he employs his mouth both to pardon and be pardoned. In short, the trust in professional skill which abounds in the General Prologue is seriously undermined in the tales: "aventure," whether it resides in under-mastery or over-mastery or mere irresponsible chance, governs them all.

The Yeoman, of course, confines his insights to his own craft. He leaves his master puzzled ("There was defaute in

somwhat"), and still embroiled in particulars ("Another
seyde the fir was over-hoot—") which will forever remain
unsettled, for the Yeoman turns now to authoritative generalization:

But, be it hoot or coold, I dar seye this,
That we concluden everemoore amys.
We faille of that which that we wolden have,
And in oure madnesse everemoore we rave.
And whan we been togidres everichon,
Every man semeth a Salomon.
But al thyng which that shineth as the gold
Nis nat gold, as that I have herd told;
Ne every appul that is fair at eye
Ne is nat good, what so men clappe or crye.
Right so, lo, fareth it amonges us:
He that semeth the wisest, by Jhesus!
Is moost fool, whan it cometh to the preef;
And he that semeth trewest is a theef.   (G969)

The movement of these lines is most interesting. The Yeoman
begins with his standard refrain, "we faille," whose implications seem to me to deepen each time he utters it, since each
time it has been strengthened with more specific evidence.
Here there is a fine contrast between the absolute singleness
of the explosion scene (which has moved from "ful ofte it
happeth" [G906] and a series of present verbs implying
frequency to past-tense verbs [G922-55] which evoke one
particular event) and the absolute generality of the twice-
repeated "everemoore." One feels convinced that the Yeoman's experience has earned him the right to make these
statements. But as he goes on his voice begins to sound
hollower: "every man semeth a Salomon" introduces a
slightly clerkish frame of reference, which comes to prevail
utterly in the succession of proverbs on gold, apples, wise
fools. This hollow note is especially evident in the line "Nis
nat gold, as that I have herd told" because of the jingle, and

because the second half of the line is both a tag and a damaging admission that the Yeoman is reaching now beyond his own experience, repeating conventional wisdom secondhand. There is an irony, furthermore, in his sounding Solomon-like himself just as he accuses others of seeming Solomons. One may rightly wonder if he himself is "moost fool" for lapsing into bromides.[9] The Canon, in contrast, has his eye upon the object: his "ther was defaute in somwhat" stands out in its particularity, its focus on the actual alone, between his fellow's exemplum of the merchant and the Yeoman's proverbs.

The Yeoman's lapse is not to be thought of as accidental or unconscious, on the Yeoman's part or Chaucer's. Having abandoned the Canon's experimental world, the Yeoman is perfectly ready to deal in conventional truisms. But in assigning them to him Chaucer accentuates the distance between him and the Canon, and maintains a balanced presentation of both the way of experience and the way of authority. And yet, for all the deep appeal we can see in the account of the Canon, it is the Yeoman's way, the way of authority, which has the victory here. This is so largely because he joins the pilgrimage and speaks, becomes an "author," while the Canon rides off. By a nice irony, the tale portrays, as the Second Nun's Tale does, a successful alchemy: through the medium of the community of pilgrims, the Yeoman, unlikely material indeed, is transmuted into gold, returned to the gay freedom he once enjoyed.

Of course, mere speaking does not make one altogether authoritative, as we quickly realize if we compare this tale to the Merchant's. Both tellers speak out of bitter experience and with an aim to discredit the institution which has embittered them. Both are also displeased with their own gullibility. But the Merchant's bitterness is indiscriminate and unmitigated: there seems no limit to his contempt for January, for himself, and for marriage, and insufficient judgment in his mixture of contempt and pity for May. Consequently he speaks of marriage with no authority. The Yeoman, for the very reason that he is able to distinguish between his master's sins and those of the second canon, and can still enter with some sympathy into the experimental world, and indeed for the very reason that as he attempts to describe that world we sense his relative ignorance of its aims and methods, speaks genuinely and sincerely. The sincerity of his sense of loss, and of his newfound freedom, has an appeal still deeper than that of the Canon. Of course, we also accept his authority because the institution he attacks is held suspect by the society to begin with, whereas in attacking marriage the Merchant can hardly expect success, particularly in this poem.

The Canon's Yeoman's Tale is a major step towards closure. On the surface it seems to thwart closure by emphasizing the open-endedness of the poem: if new members can join the pilgrimage, we can go on forever. But on reflection one sees that it has the opposite effect: everything about it suggests we are near the end. It could hardly have come near the beginning, where the proximity of the General Prologue is still palpable; the author can only feel the occasion for these fresh recruits if the dominance of the Prologue has waned. And yet clearly the poem cannot tolerate a series of new characters without seriously damaging its inner coherence. If we sense that, then we must sense that we are near the end, since only if the poem is near the end, and therefore further such intrusions are unlikely, can it safely afford the risk of one. Inwardly, the substance of the tale, and its tone, similarly smack of ending. Most notable here is the Yeoman's constantly raising the very issue of "conclusion." His stress on the failure to reach conclusion may cause us to reflect on conclusion in general and on conclusion of this poem in particular. The elegiac tone, the laments over loss, the skepticism about craft, and the realization that the Yeoman has, after all, come to a conclusion of a way of life—all intensify the sense of imminent closure. So too does the theme of conversion, particularly as it is carried over from the Second Nun's Tale; it reminds us of the goal of the pilgrimage. And above all the examination and rejection of an eccentric mode of experience, with a concomitant "centric" move by the Yeoman toward the community and its norm, make it less likely that the poem can continue its free exploration of various worlds. No personal expression of this quality has yet taken place on the pilgrimage: the squabbles and chatter are trivial in comparison; even the startling marital confessions of the Host, the Merchant, and the Wife involve no present change, only revelation of the past (though a sensitive listener might divine that the Wife grows as she talks); only the Pardoner's "collection" and what follows it can match the Yeoman's conversion as a significant present event, but it is slight in comparison to the major change the Yeoman undergoes in the presence of the pilgrims, and then validates by his tale. After such knowledge, the poem seems less able to turn away from the solemn spiritual issues that have seemed deferable but never finally dismissible.[10]

The Manciple's Tale does not break the newly solemn tone, and makes its own contributions toward closure. The solemn tone, and the sense of ending, are powerful enough to turn the traditionally comic matter of adultery into material for tragedy—where Alison escaped scot-free, Apollo's wife dies—and to raise serious questions about the value of speaking, or telling tales, at all.[11] The crow, indeed, is another Chaucer:

> countrefete the speche of every man
> He koude, whan he sholde telle a tale.   (H135)

But the crow is reduced to inarticulacy, and Chaucer also is ready for silence, ready, as Apollo does, to "break his minstralsy." Then comes the Parson's Prologue, so full of the sense of ending, and the Parson's Tale itself, which is explicitly skeptical about poetry and about fictions, and elegiac in its sense of the sinfulness of man, and so turns for hope to a vision of heaven. To it we must now turn.

146

7. Closure II: the Parson's Tale and Chaucer's Retraction

The Parson's Tale makes most readers close the book before the book closes. And yet a thorough response to the poem obviously must include a sensitive understanding of the Parson's Tale; there is little use in supposing, as many seem to, that Chaucer tossed it in because he had it lying around. Rather, in a variety of ways it can be seen to knit up the feast with fine decorum.

Above all, it is the climax of the movement in the direction of oneness that we have seen implicit thematically through the whole multiple middle of the poem, and becoming more explicit in groups G and H. Like them it focuses on conclusion, on death and silence, and it leads to Chaucer's consideration of his own death before it lapses into silence. In larger terms, it stands, like the General Prologue, in a relation of one to many to the tales. They are particular, it is general. It is even general in relation to the General Prologue. The tales are "storial thyng," it is revelatory; that is, its relation to the tales is comparable to the relation of Revelation to the narrative books of the Bible.[1] It transforms physical themes of the tales into their spiritual counterparts. And it is an authoritative choice of "one way," where the tales are tolerant and experimental—though the major values it settles for are in fact the values of some of the tales. Finally, it constitutes a Christian counterpart to the "pagan" version of oneness presented in the Knight's Tale.

147

The One and the Many

Before taking up these topics more fully, I wish simply to describe the Parson's Tale and indicate what values it promotes. It has two distinct parts: a treatise on penitence and, embedded in that, a treatise on the Seven Deadly Sins. The two are quite different. The penitence part deals with the relationship between man and God; consequently, its imagery and outlook are spiritual and transcendent. The treatise on the deadly sins, since all of them are practiced with or against other people, and since their sinfulness lies, one way or another, in injury to other people, deals with relationships among people. This distinction means that the two parts bear different relations to the rest of the poem: in general, in the penitence part one finds the Parson transforming the issues and imagery of the tales into spiritual terms, whereas the sins part frequently seems to "quite" the implied values of the General Prologue, as well as to insist on the values of certain tales. But the distinction is not rigid: both relations are discernible in both parts.

The Parson's Tale is a vision of perfect community or oneness, on two levels: here on earth and in heaven. Both are brought about by a double communion, between men and men, and between men and God. Communion with God is paramount, and the theme of the penitence part. Sin is separation from God; by it "we wrathe oure Lord Jhesu Crist" (110). From the "roote" of contrition, however, "spryngeth a seed of grace . . . and this seed is egre and hoot" (117).

> The heete of this seed is the love of God, and the desiryng of the joye perdurable. This heete draweth the herte of man to God. . . . The synful man that loveth his synne, hym semeth that it is to him moost sweete of anythyng; but fro that tyme that he loveth sadly oure Lord Jhesu Crist, and desireth the lif perdurable, ther nys to him no thyng moore abhomynable. (121, 124)

Sin merits hell, which is the absence of God: "he that is in helle

Closure II: the Parson's Tale and Chaucer's Retraction

shal have defaute of the sighte of God; for certes, the sighte of
God is the lyf perdurable" (184). The heavenly communion is
symbolized by a feast, like that held for the prodigal son by
his father (701):

> "I was atte dore of thyn herte," seith Jhesus, "and cleped
> for to entre. He that openeth to me shall have foryifnesse
> of synne. I wol entre into hym by my grace, and soupe
> with hym," by the goode werkes that he shal doon,
> whiche werkes been the foode of God; "and he shal
> soupe with me."   (290)

This communion joins one finally not only with God but on
earth with "the compaignye and communyoun of holy chirche" (312) and in heaven with the communion of saints. The
"fruyt" of penance is "the endelees blisse of hevene," "ther as
is the blisful compaignye that rejoysen hem everemo, everich
of otheres joye . . . ther as ne is neither hunger, thurst, ne
coold, but every soule replenyssed with the sighte of the
parfit knowynge of God" (1076-79). The major way in which
the Parson "knits up all this feast" is to focus consideration on
this spiritual company and its feast of joyful knowing; as he
transforms the "wey" into that of the "parfit glorious pilgrymage / That highte Jerusalem celestial," he transforms the
"soper at oure aller cost" into supping with Christ, thereby
suggesting that the tales are not a competition for a prize but a
mutual feeding, the pilgrims not rivals but a company, taking
bread together from each other and especially from this
pastor. As the Host's plan is diminished in number, it is
transformed in nature.

The Parson's vision of communion appears also in less
transcendent, more human and earthly terms. He emphasizes
friendship again and again. Hell entails not only separation
from God but "defaute of frendes" (199). Envy is "the worste
synne that is" because "it is sory of alle the bountees of his
neighebor" (488-89); through discord it "unbyndeth alle manere of frendshipe" (511). The remedy to envy is love of both

149

God and neighbor, "for soothly, that oon ne may nat ben withoute that oother. And truste wel that in the name of thy neighebor thou shalt understonde the name of thy brother; for certes alle we have o fader flesshly, and o moder, that is to seyn, Adam and Eve; and eek o fader spirituel that is God of hevene. Thy neighebor artow holden for to love" (514-17).[2] Wrath engenders "chidynge and reproche," which "unsowen the semes of frendshipe in mannes herte" (622). Christ died "to make concord. . . . For God loveth bettre that frendshipe be amonges folk, than he dide his owene body, which that he yaf for unitee" (642-43). Sloth breeds "a manere cooldnesse, that freseth al the herte of man" (722). Adultery breaks the community of husband and wife, makes many what was one: it "kerveth atwo and breketh atwo hem that first were maked o flessh" (888); and it undermines the basis of community among men in general: from it follows "brekynge of feith; and certes, in feith is the keye of Cristendom" (875).

The broader community of men in general is envisioned as a hierarchical society based on good will and mutual service. The hierarchy is not natural, it is the product of original sin: "thise lordes ne sholde nat muche glorifien hem in hir lord-shipes, sith that by naturel condicion they ben nat lordes over thralles, but that thraldom comth first by the desert of synne" (757). The Redemption did not rid the world of rank, but instead imposed on those in command an obligation of service in imitation of Christ: "sith the time of grace cam, God ordeyned that som folk sholde be moore heigh in estaat and in degree, and som folk moore lough, and that everich sholde be served in his estaat" (771). "The lord oweth to his man that the man oweth to his lord" (772). Sovereignty was ordained only because without it "the commune profit myghte nat han be kept, ne pees and rest in erthe" (773). This ideal of community is applied to economic as well as political life: "there as God hath ordeyned that a regne or a contree is suffisaunt to hymself, thanne is it honest and leveful that of habundaunce of this contree, that men helpe another contree that is moore nedy" (778). There runs through the tale a strong thread of sympathy for members of the community who are ordinarily neglected: servants, children, the poor. The proper functioning of the community depends on order, on all levels: in the cosmos, between God and man, in society, and in the individual person. "God hath creat alle thynges in right ordre, and no thyng withouten ordre, but alle thynges ben ordeyned and nombred" (218). Man must be "obeisaunt to God, that is his lord" (338), and to his earthly lord as well: "obedience generally is to perfourne the doctrine of God and of his sovereyns" (676). As for the inner self, "God, and reson, and sensualitee, and the body of man ben so ordeyned that everich of thise foure thynges sholde have lordshipe over that oother" (261); but "whan man synneth, al this ordre or ordinaunce is turned up-so-doun" (263). The passion of Christ was a kind of superimposition of a new order of service by God to man, to counteract the disorder brought about by sin: "this disordinaunce and this rebellioun oure Lord Jhesu Crist aboghte" (267); "after the diverse disordinaunces of oure wikkednesses was the passioun of Jhesu Crist ordeyned in diverse thynges" (275). Inner order is also stressed in the constant call to "mesure."

As for social rank and degree, although its importance is granted, as we have seen, for the sake of peace, it gives way not only to the theory of equal responsibility of lord and man in service, but to a hierarchy of virtue. All men are born free; the only true thraldom is the thraldom of sin: "wel oghte man have desdayn of synne, sith that thurgh synne, ther he was free, now is he maked bonde" (149).

> Allas! wel oghten they thanne have desdayn to ben servauntz and thralles to synne, and soore ben ashamed of hemself, that God of his endelees goodnesse hath set hem in heigh estaat, or yeven hem wit, strengthe of body, heele, beautee, prosperitee, and boghte hem fro the deeth with his herte-blood, that they so unkyndely, agayns his gentilesse, quiten hym so vileynsly to slaughtre of hir owene soules. (154)

As Seneca says, "'I am born to gretter thynges than to be thral to my body, or than for to maken of my body a thral'" (145). "O manere gentrye is for to preise, that apparailleth mannes corage with vertues and moralitees, and maketh hym Cristes child" (462). "Gentillesse" is "a man to have a noble herte and a diligent (i.e., loving), to attayne to heighe vertuouse thynges" (469). And yet every man is a prisoner, too, since concupiscence makes some disorder inevitable. Saint Paul realized that flesh and spirit "'so stryven that a man may nat alway doon as he wolde'" (342), and cried, "'Allas, I caytyf man! who shal delivere me fro the prison of my caytyf body?'" (344).

The Parson's Tale, then, presents a complex vision of man as bound both to God and to other men in a relationship of service and love, and enjoying the community which this relation brings about when its elements are set in proper order—a community of free men who are most free, most "in heigh estaat," when they act responsibly and lovingly toward each other. But the vision recognizes also the fragility of the community, its tendency to disorder and disruption, arising out of the innate tendency in all men to forfeit their high estate for servitude to sin. It is perhaps in view of this contradictory vision of the innate goodness and innate wickedness of man that the virtue most consistently praised is "patient suffraunce."[3] The model for this, of course, is Christ: "heer-agayns (i.e., against "outrageous labour in werkes") suffred Crist ful paciently and taughte us pacience, whan he baar upon his blissed shulder the croys upon which he sholde suffren despitous deth" (668). Christ's great act of goodness required him to place himself in a "despitous" position: he was highest when he was lowliest. Patient sufferance expresses the paradox in man because it combines his lowliness with his "birth to higher things." It also contains an implicit acknowledgment not only that men are cruel to one another but that despite the various gifts of nature, fortune, and grace (cf. 450ff.) with which men are endowed, they suffer inevitable adversity: patient sufferance not only "suffreth swetely alle the anoyaunces and the wronges that men doon to man outward" (656), but "suffreth debonairely alle the outrages of adversitee" (660). It is further humane in that it is not restricted to Christianity: "noght oonly Cristen men ben pacient ... but certes, the olde payens that nevere were Cristene commendeden and useden the vertu of pacience" (669). But it is not merely human: "this vertu maketh a man lyk to God" (661). It thus promotes community between man and God, as it does between man and man ("if thow wolt venquysse thyn enemy, lerne to suffre" [661]),[4] and even between man and woman ("a man sholde bere hym with his wif . . . in suffraunce and in reverence" [925]). The exhortation to patient sufferance runs through the tale like a refrain.[5]

I have dwelt at length on what the Parson's Tale says because it is too often dismissed as "a treatise on the Seven Deadly Sins," which it is not, or "a treatise on penance," a more accurate phrase which still does little justice to its intricacy, its fulness, and its positive vision of man and his purpose. Having described that positive vision, we are now in a position to analyze the role of the Parson's Tale in bringing the *Canterbury Tales* to a close. In a sentence, that role is to make the final movement from many to one. This movement is accomplished—paradoxically enough—in many ways. The major way, of course, is through the emphasis on God, who is the One (though not called that here). And my summary indicates the Parson's repeated emphasis on unity: on the way, "the goode wey" (77), "the righte wey of Jerusalem celestial" (80); on the community of men, and on what unites God and man; on the soul single-mindedly bent on salvation. But above all it is in its relation to the other tales that we can see most clearly how the Parson's Tale moves from many to one, and from particular to general.

First, it should be pointed out that the Parson's Tale is not altogether *sui generis*: it belongs to the class of professional tales, and like many of them it "quites" the tale of a rival professional; it also bears a close relation to the portrait of the teller in the General Prologue. It belongs to the professional group of tales in which the teller reveals his own craft: the Wife's Prologue, the Pardoner's Tale, and the Canon's Yeoman's Tale. The Parson's job is to save souls, and in his tale he shows us, directly, how he does it: like the Pardoner, he gives an exemplary sermon. He also teaches us the art of repentance. The Parson's two professional rivals on the pilgrimage are the Pardoner and the Friar: the Pardoner because he visits country churches and makes off with donations which rightly should go to the parson, making "the person and the peple his apes" (A706); the Friar because he usurps the power of confession and extracts money in return for easy absolution, as we learn both in the General Prologue and in the Summoner's Tale. And both are preachers. The Parson's Tale should be thought of as "quiting" both these figures—subtly and implicitly, in accordance with the Parson's style—because it is an honest sermon aimed genuinely at repentance.[6] This professional purpose is the basic dimension of the tale, not to be forgotten as we explore its moral role. At base the Parson is, like the others, skillful at his job and jealous of its prerogatives; in his sermon he asserts these prerogatives implicitly by doing his job well. The Host has recognized them by granting him the final word. (We may hear, too, an echo of the "professional" opposition between clerks and wives; the "wey," of which the Parson knows so much, and speaks so straightforwardly, is opposed utterly to the Wife and all she knows of "wandrynge by the weye".)

The relation of the tale to the portrait of the Parson in the General Prologue is specific and demonstrable. It puts on display the Parson's richness of holy thought and his learning, and as an action it is a holy work. It is a true preaching and devout teaching of Christ's gospel, which it quotes constantly and which is the source of its major ideas. The virtues ascribed to the Parson in the portrait—benignity, diligence, patience in adversity, perseverance in good works, "suffisaunce" in "litel thyng," lack of disdain and harsh speech toward sinners, lack of pomp—all are the very virtues to which he returns again and again in the tale (cf., e.g., 405, 518,

626-30, 660, 679, 713, 720, 734, 833). He harps also on the distinction, made in the portrait, between word and work—the need for both but the greater emphasis on work (this is everywhere; see, e.g., 109-110, 478, 518-20, 1045-46, and especially 650, 689, 736). Lines 785-92 speak of simony, and the selling of prayers, in terms similar to those of the General Prologue: "They sellen the soules that lambes sholde kepen (i.e., they who should keep lambs sell the lambs' souls) to the wolf that strangleth hem" (792). Similarly, of those who do not persevere in good work, "Thise ben the newe sheepherdes that leten hir sheep wityngly go renne to the wolf that is in the breres, or do no fors of hir owene governaunce" (721). For the sharp snubbing of obstinate sinners (A523), cf. 583-85: "whan a man is sharply amonested in his shrifte to forleten synne, thanne wole he be angry, and answeren hokerly and angrily . . . ." On visiting (A491-95), see: "a man hath nede of . . . visitynge in prisone and in maladie" (1031). Finally, the Parson is consistent in his plainness. His straightforward language—"a shiten shepherde and a clene sheep" (these words, though Chaucer's, are implicitly the Parson's; cf. A498-99)—and his dislike of pomp and "a spiced conscience" find their counterpart in his prologue in his disdain for "rum, ram, ruf" and rhyme and fables, his "I wol nat glose," and in the tale itself not only in the plain style but in specific condemnation of such things as "outrageous apparailynge of mete" (833) or "delicat ese" (835), or painting one's confession "by faire subtile wordes" (1022). "Tellen it platly," he urges.[7]

This insistence on flatness not only constitutes a major element in the suiting of tale to teller; it is also a key element in the contrast of the Parson to the Pardoner and the Friar. Both Pardoner and Friar are inveterate "glosers" and "peynters"; among the Pardoner's complexities is his self-awareness, his ability to stand back from himself and say, "Lo, sires, thus I preche." The Parson shows the pilgrims how he preaches also, but he does so directly, by preaching sincerely to them.

Thus even his participation in the standard professional rivalry of the poem is done in a unified and integrated way; in him word and act are one; his whole being is integrated. The professional character of his tale is a "particular" aspect of it, but not one that associates him with multiplicity.

Thus the Parson's Tale is general because the general categories of "professionalism" and "fitness to the teller" include it. It is further general in that it is expository, not narrative. It has no particular characters. In this way, too, it is "plat" where the other tales are "spiced." Here we have unadorned truth; everywhere else, in the General Prologue and the other tales, there is the "spice" of verse or fiction or both. One very large aspect of the relation of the Parson's Tale to the rest of the poem is that it replaces literary truth with moral truths, asserting implicitly that this general mode of discourse is more effective than that particular mode.

If the Parson's Tale is to provide full closure, we might expect it to bear a special relation to the General Prologue: to end generally as that began generally, to be a kind of general epilogue. I shall argue that it is just that, and that this is an important way that it is general. Its relation to the General Prologue is teasing and complex, but essential to explore if we are to uncover its full role. In the first place, both the General Prologue and the Parson's sermon clearly derive from the same satiric tradition, as details such as women who insist on being first to bring their offering suggest.[8] The General Prologue, however, while still often satirical, employs this material in an objective or even benevolent fashion, accepting things such as money, clothing, speech, and social intercourse as the irreducible givens of human existence, the materials out of which life and character are created, having no particular moral dimension. What the Parson does is assign, or reassign, a moral dimension to these materials, and explore the dark side of the bright world of the General Prologue. This is particularly evident in the penitence portion, in the Parson's long account of hell (178-230)—which explicates Job 10:20-22, quoted at 176-77—and in his whole treatment of the deadly sins.

Closure II: the Parson's Tale and Chaucer's Retraction

Hell is, in Job's phrase, a "lond of mysese" (177, 186), whereas at the Tabard "wel we weren esed atte beste." The world of the General Prologue is brightened and warmed by the "cheere" of the Tabard and the dayspring, and by the all-seeing eye of the narrator as well. Hell is "the derke lond, covered with the derknesse of deeth" (176), wherein a man's sins "destourben hym to see the face of God, right as a derk clowde bitwixe us and the sonne" (185). In hell "ther ben three maneres of defautes, agayn three thynges that folk of this world han in this present lyf, that is to seyn, honours, delices, and richesses" (186). The General Prologue is saturated with these three things, particularly "richesses."

Hell replaces riches with "mysese of poverte" (192ff.), which consists of the lack of four things: treasure, meat and drink, clothing, and friendship, the last including sexual love. But money, food, clothing, friendship, and sex are the staple images of the General Prologue. Similarly, the "delices" of the five senses (207ff.) will be replaced in hell by darkness, wailing, stink, gall, and quenchless fire; one is reminded of the multiple appeal to the senses in the General Prologue, particularly by images of color, music, and food. The trenchant account of hell, in short, presents a kind of underbelly to the General Prologue. It does not undermine it or question its values directly; in fact, it corrobates those values by accepting them as the "thynges that folk of this world han in this present lyf" (186), and increases their appeal by imagining the pain of life without them. But it clearly does imply that some larger conception of human life is demanded, not only because these goods eventually vanish, but because in most cases it is delighting in them that will bring one to hell: the rich will be poor *because* they "oneden al hire herte to tresor of this world" (193); they will be naked because, despite "the gaye robes, and the softe shetes, and the smale shertes," their souls are naked "of alle manere vertues, which that is the clothyng of soule" (197). Sex, too, will earn them hell: "hire flesshly love was deedly hate, as seith the prophete David: 'Whoso that loveth wikkednesse, he hateth his soule'"

157

(204). Thus despite its acknowledgment that these pleasures
are the ordinary stuff of life in this world, the passage by
strong implication questions the very values which the General Prologue accepts so cheerfully. "Whoso thanne wolde
wel understande thise peynes . . . he sholde have moore talent
to siken and to wepe, than for to syngen and to pleye" (228).

The treatise on the Seven Deadly Sins bears a similar,
though less concentrated, relation to the General Prologue.
Scattered throughout it are remarks that find fault with things
taken for granted in the General Prologue. "Outrageous array
of clothyng" is attacked under Pride (412), "a likerousnesse in
herte to have erthely thynges" under Avarice (741), "to delicat
mete or drynke" under Gluttony (828), disordinate love
under Lechery. Many details recall specific portraits: "super-
fluitee or . . . inordinat scantnesse of [clothynge]" (414) recalls
the Squire's "short . . . gowne, with sleves longe and wyde"
(A93); "costlewe furrynge in hire gownes" (418) and "to
manye delicat horses that ben holden for delit" (432) recall
the Monk; "pride of the table" (444) and "excesse of diverse
metes and drynkes" (445), the Franklin; simony (781), the
Friar and the Summoner; lechery in priests (891), the Monk
and the Friar; jangling (406), the Miller.[9]

The Wife of Bath can be thought of as conceived in direct
opposition to the Parson's opinions. (This is a subtle aspect of
the general opposition between them.) She earns her living
making cloth, and her portrait mentions seven different items
of clothing—kerchiefs, hose, shoes, wimple, hat, foot-man-
tle, and spurs,—most of which are hardly "measurable." The
proud man wants to "goon to offryng biforn his neighebor"
(407), and "he that is proud or envyous is lightly wrooth"
(534); when seeking forgiveness it is essential "that thow be
nat out of charitee" (1043). Yet

In al the parisshe wif ne was ther noon
That to the offrynge bifore hire sholde goon;
And if ther dide, certeyn so wrooth was she,
That she was out of alle charitee.   (A452)

158

Closure II: the Parson's Tale and Chaucer's Retraction

She hardly exhibits "patient suffraunce." She has followed neither of the "two maneres" of restraining the ardor of lust, "chastitee in mariage and chastitee of widwehod" (916), nor, whether in youth or on pilgrimage, the injunction to "eschue the compaignye of hem by whiche he douteth to be tempted" (953); rather she is one of the "lovynge children" (202).[10] So far from seeking community with Christ or holy church, she seeks fellowship where she can "laughe and carpe": she is a "talker of ydel wordes" (378), she "speketh to muche biforn folk" (406). As a "worthy (i.e., rich) womman al hir lyve," she shows "a likerousnesse in herte to have erthely thynges" (741).
In short she is the very opposite of the Parson's ideal: "Thise manere wommen that observen chastitee moste be clene in herte as wel as in body and in thought, and mesurable in clothynge and in contenaunce (cf. "boold was hir face"), abstinent in etynge and drynkynge, in spekynge, and in dede" (947). ⊂ 1̲ Tim.

To sum up the relation of the Parson's Tale to the General Prologue, then, one can say that both are built out of the same material: men and women in their relation to the ordinary objects and activities of life: food, clothing, money, fellowship, sex. In the General Prologue these categories are diffused into the particular descriptions of the dress and habits of particular representative people, made with little or no moral judgment; in the Parson's Tale the general categories are reconstituted and placed in a clear moral framework. The two modes fit the respective roles of these two parts of the poem: the mode of the General Prologue is "open," it generates further interplay among the pilgrims and further ground for moral judgment; the mode of the Parson's Tale is closed and closural. By putting the parts back together into a structure, and by placing that structure on a moral frame, it makes for finality. Both are general, but the Parson's Tale is far more general.

The Parson's Tale also generalizes from the body of the poem. It does so by placing into its large moral context of sin and forgiveness most or all of the major issues that arise in

159

particular contexts in the Tales. It would take too much space to list all the specific parallels between the Parson's Tale and the other tales,[11] but a brief indication may be in order here. Again I shall use the treatise on the Seven Deadly Sins. The Parson's account of each of the sins contains parallels to several tales. Under Pride, compare the injunction against jangling (406) to the Manciple's Tale and ClT E1200; the discourse on "gentillesse" to WBT and to Theseus; the remarks on Fortune to KnT, and especially 472 to KnT A1255-56 and PardT C547-48; the remarks on the brittleness of popularity to ClT E995ff., SqT F221-24; the injunction to assent to good counsel to *Melibee.* Under Envy, cf. the Reeve, the Pardoner, and the Wife; compare 484 to PhysT C114-16; on "gruchchyng" (499), cf. KnT, especially A3057ff.; on suffering patiently, Grisilde; on "whan men discovereth a mannes harm that was pryvee, or bereth hym on hond thyng that is fals" (505), the Wife; on loving one's enemy, *Melibee.* Under Wrath, see especially SummT D1981-2093, *Melibee* B2311ff., and the Reeve, the Pardoner, and the friar in the SummT; on judicial vengeance (571-72), *Melibee* B2623ff.; on swearing, PardT C629-59, of which ParsT 587-600 is the direct source; cf. also ML endlink B1171; on conjuring (602ff.), cf. PardT C350ff., and John the carpenter; on flatterers "that syngen evere *Placebo*" (617), cf. MerchT, SummT D2075, and *Melibee;* on cursing that "retorneth agayn to hym that curseth" (620), cf. FrT; on chiding (622), cf. MancT, and on chiding in marriage (631ff.), cf. the Wife, especially WBP D278-80, 777, and *Melibee* B2276; on counsel, *Melibee;* on those who "maken semblant as though they speke ... in game and pley" (644), cf. the Cook, A4354-55, NPT B4452, and FranklT F988; on the remedy for ire, patient sufferance, cf. MLT, ClT, and *Melibee.* Under Sloth, cf. SNT Prol and KnT A1940. The Reeve and the Pardoner may be guilty of *tristicia,* when "a man is anoyed of his owene lif" (726); its remedy is "constaunce" (737), cf. MLT. Under Avarice, cf. PardT; on "harde lordshipes" (752-64), cf. ClT; on the equality of churls and lords (761ff.), cf. WBT, and on their equality in death

160

(762), cf. KnT A3030 and MLT B1142; on extortion of the Church (767), cf. FrT; on fraudulent "marchandise" (780), ShipT; on hazardry (793ff.), PardT C589ff.; on the remedy for Avarice, "pitee," cf. KnT, SqT, FranklT, etc. Under Gluttony, cf. PardT C483-588, of which the Parson's passage is the source; on gluttony as Adam and Eve's sin (819), PardT C505-11, SummT D1915-16. Under Lechery, on its relation to gluttony (836), cf. MLT B925-31, PardT C481ff., and WBP D466; on its relation to the flood (839), cf. MillT; on sex and money (849), cf. WBP and ShipT; for the phrase "a foul thyng . . . a fouler" (849), cf. PardT C524-25; for the image of a merchant who "deliteth hym moost in chaffare that he hath moost avantage of" (851), cf. ShipT; for "olde dotardes holours" (857), cf. WBP, MerchT; for those who think they cannot sin in marriage (859), cf. MerchT E1838-41; on virginity as the highest degree (868), cf. WBP; on the impossibility of restoring maidenhead (871), cf. MLProl B30; on bawds (886), cf. FriarT; on unchaste clerics (891ff.), the Monk, the Friar, and ShipT; on Christ at Cana (919), cf. WBP; on marriage replenishing the church (920), cf. WBP D71-72; on women and maistrie (927ff.), cf. all the marriage tales, especially WBP, WBT, ClT, and FranklT; on Christ's virginity (950), cf. WBP 139; on eschewing tempting company (953), cf. WBP passim.

Thus there is hardly a tale whose themes and ethos are untouched by the Parson's Tale, and some of the major tales—Knight's, Man of Law's, *Melibee*, Wife of Bath's Prologue and Tale, Pardoner's, Clerk's, Merchant's—seem especially closely tied to it. Issues diffused here and there through the tales, many of them the source of disagreement, are here united within a single authoritative moral framework. The values of the Man of Law's Tale, *Melibee*, and the Clerk's Tale—constancy, forgiveness, patient suffering, obedience, "reverence" between husband and wife—are vigorously and consistently corroborated; the lechery, fraud, malice, avarice, and other vices that many tales feature are roundly condemned. The relation to the Wife's Prologue and to the Pardoner's Tale is complex; both these speakers draw much material directly from the Parson's Tale, but use it idiosyncratically.

The Parson's Tale gives the structure of the entire poem a rough relationship to the structure of the Bible: a long, complex history told in a series of individual parts, and framed by Genesis and Revelation. The General Prologue describes the "birth" of the pilgrimage. It opens with images of new generation, and its relation to the rest of the poem is not only general but generative; the interrelations of pilgrims, and the Host's creative suggestion, bring about the body of the poem. The Parson's Tale, like Revelation, marks a sudden transcendence into a new sphere: it looks to the future and the life beyond; it is eschatological and magisterial, the product of a vision different in kind from the "historical" vision of the narratives that have gone before it. The parallel is reinforced by the Parson's own account of the "three estates" of man: "th'estaat of innocence, as was th'estaat of Adam biforn that he fil into synne. . . . The estaat of synful men. . . . Th'estaat of grace" (682-84). In the poem the relatively innocent air of the General Prologue—arising from the sense of beginning, the freshness of our sense of the pilgrims despite various suspect details in the descriptions, the happy fellowship, and the narrator's eager approval—is replaced by a fallen world of conflict, sordid confession, venal and animal interests; but this is in turn replaced by the call to the "lif perdurable" by the Parson.

This sudden transcendence is especially marked in the penance portion. The sins portion, though more general and authoritative, has a direct relationship to the tales, as the extensive parallels I have just instanced suggest. In the penance portion, ideas and images in the tales are consistently transformed into a new and more spiritual plane.

This transformation begins in the Parson's Prologue,[12] perhaps even as early as its opening lines, wherein even the physical description of the time of day seems to stretch beyond the mundane and solid world, with its focus on the narrator's eleven-foot shadow and its talk of descent and ascent, of "exaltacioun," of ending and fulfillment. The Parson speaks of tale-telling in the potent biblical metaphor of sowing wheat ("Why sholde I sowen draf out of my fest, / Whan I may sowen whete?" 35-36), transforming the ordinary "sentence and solas" into "plesaunce leefful"—such pleasure as is allowed "at Cristes reverence," its full implications including "the joy that comes from fulfilling the law." Since his tale will "knytte up al this feeste, and make an ende," it replaces, as I have said, the "soper at oure aller cost" that we were led originally to expect at the end. This metaphor of a feast of reason, or of spirit, carries on the image of spiritual food introduced by "whete" and forms one of the major images of the tale, that of spiritual fructuousness, culminating in the image of supping eternally with Christ (287-91). It is also the ultimate transformation not only of the many food images in the General Prologue, but of various eating scenes in the tales, such as those of the Man of Law, Shipman, Nuns' Priest, Summoner, Clerk, Merchant, Squire, and Pardoner. Similarly, the Parson transforms another master image—*the* master image, in fact—that of the pilgrims' road, into "the wey . . . / Of thilke parfit glorious pilgrymage / That highte Jerusalem celestial" (49-51). These simple transformations have an immediate effect on the spirit of the company of pilgrims, and on the Host. The universal assent they express has not appeared since the original supper at the Tabard, or perhaps since the first cut fell to the Knight. Nor has the Host since then spoken with such universal authority: he "hadde the wordes for us alle" (67). And his words suggest a new spirit of acquiescence and benevolence in him: he blesses the Parson as he has no other pilgrim, and prays for God's grace on him to do well.

In the tale itself the transformations of major issues and images continue. Thraldom (including both imprisonment and servitude) and freedom, a central matter in at least a dozen tales,[13] including all the marriage tales, is now a matter of the soul, not the body. Judgment, an issue not only in tales such as *Melibee* and the Physician's Tale but in the Host's and the other pilgrims' critical response to all the tales, now focuses on the day of doom (158ff.)[14] For marriage we have a new knitting with God, or "the knyttynge togidre of Crist and of holy chirche" (843). Sex, a physical matter, largely disappears: most of the Parson's statements apply to any "soul," not to male or female. The dichotomy of male and female is "knit up." The consistent concern for "entente" appears in the form of consent to sin; "telling" in general, and the impulse toward confession in particular, are sacramentalized, as is the notion of reconciliation, a constant issue both in tales and among pilgrims; various *amores* are subsumed in the love of God. The opening image of the poem, that of the "flour" of spring, is reinterpreted in spiritual terms:

> *Nazarenus* is as muche for to seye as "florisshynge," in which a man shal hope that he that yeveth hym remissioun of synnes shal yeve hym eek grace wel to do. For in the flour is hope of fruyt in tyme comynge, and in foryifnesse of synnes hope of grace wel to do.   (288)

The notion of transformation itself has been a regular issue in the poem, occurring most specifically in the Wife of Bath's Tale and the Canon's Yeoman's Tale. The relation of the latter to the Parson's Tale is particularly strong though not atypical; it can serve as an example of how the Parson's Tale transforms earlier physical matters into matters of the spirit. The Parson's Tale concerns the art of repentance or spiritual alchemy: how to transform the soul dulled by sin into the soul renewed and made precious by grace. "Soothly, the goode werkes that he dide biforn that he fil in synne ben al mortefied and astoned and dulled by the ofte synnyng" (233). But these works "quyken agayn . . . and availlen to have the lyf perdurable in hevene, whan we han contricioun" (241). Good works done in sin, however, will never quicken, "for certes, thyng that nevere hadde lyf may nevere quykene" (243). In view of such mortification and lifelessness, "wel may that

man that no good werk ne dooth synge thilke newe Frenshe
song, *'Jay tout perdu mon temps et mon labour'"* *(248).* The
passage is shot through with the language of the Canon's
Yeoman's Tale: work, avail, mortify, dull, quicken, loss, debt.
The Canon gives himself over to "the work" of mortifying
and quickening; but

> oure materes that lyen al fix adoun
> Mowe in oure werkyng no thyng us availle,
> For lost is al oure labour and travaille.   (G781)

The Parson describes an alchemy of the spirit that transforms
and quickens and avails.

The following rich paragraph repeats the pattern of the
Yeoman's experience of fall and rise, of enslavement and
liberation, transforming it to a higher spiritual level:

> The seconde cause that oghte make a man to have
> desdeyn of synne is this: that, as seith Seint Peter, "whoso
> that dooth synne is thral of synne"; and synne put a man
> in greet thraldom. And therfore seith the prophete
> Ezechiel: "I wente sorweful in desdayn of myself."
> Certes, wel oghte a man have desdayn of synne, and
> withdrawe hym from that thraldom and vileynye. And
> lo, what seith Seneca in this matere? He seith thus:
> "Though I wiste that neither God ne man ne sholde
> nevere knowe it, yet wolde I have desdayn for to do
> synne." And the same Seneca also seith: "I am born to
> gretter thynges than to be thral to my body, or than for to
> maken of my body a thral." Ne a fouler thral may no man
> ne womman maken of his body than for to yeve his body
> to synne. Al were it the fouleste cherl or the fouleste
> womman that lyveth, and leest of value, yet is he thanne
> moore foul and moore in servitute. Evere fro the hyer
> degree that man falleth, the moore is he thral, and moore
> to God and to the world vile and abhomynable. O goode
> God, wel oghte man have desdayn of synne, sith that

thurgh synne, ther he was free, now is he maked bonde.
And therfore seyth Seint Augustyn: "If thou hast desdayn
of thy servant, if he agilte or synne, have thou thanne
desdayn that thou thyself sholdest do synne." Take
reward of thy value, that thou ne be to foul to thyself.
Allas! wel oghten they thanne have desdayn to ben
servauntz and thralles to synne, and soore ben ashamed
of hemself, that God of his endelees goodnesse hath set
hem in heigh estaat, or yeven hem wit, strengthe of
body, heele, beautee, prosperitee, and boghte hem fro
the deeth with his herte-blood, that they so unkyndely,
agayns his gentilesse, quiten hym so vileynsly to slaugh-
tre of hir owene soules.   (142-54)

The Yeoman has made himself the Canon's thrall, or alchemy's thrall, and in so doing made himself foul, "vile and
abhomynable." He is "discoloured of [his] face" (G664),
"wan and of a leden hewe" (G728) where he was "wont to be
right fressh and gay" (G724). When he meets the pilgrims, he
"takes regard of his value," "withdraws him from that
thraldom," removes himself from the self-slaughtering world
of alchemy. But that was all on a physical or material plane;
the Parson applies the pattern to spiritual thraldom and
release.

   Nor are the relations of this passage confined to the
Canon's Yeoman's Tale. Thraldom is a central image in the
Knight's and Monk's Tales; the Wife says a husband "shal be
bothe my dettour and my thral" (D155); the Franklin insists
conversely that "Wommen, of kynde, desiren libertee, / And
nat to been constreyned as a thral; / And so doon men"
(F768-70); Walter is bound to his compulsive purpose "right
as [he] were bounden to a stake" (E704). Many characters are
thralls to their bodies; those who consider themselves "born
to greater things" are generally "servants" like Damian or
Aurelius, wives, or poor students who desire more or greater
things (including *la bele chose*) than they have, not the
transcendence of which Seneca speaks. The pilgrims them-

selves do not understand "heigh estaat" or "gentilesse" as they are understood here; and the "wit, strengthe of body, heele, beautee, prosperitee" celebrated in the General Prologue are neither associated with redemption nor contrasted to "vileynye" in terms of the soul. The passage takes a complex mixture of major ideas from the poem and elevates them to a new spiritual plane.

The Parson's Tale also represents a clear movement from experience to authority. The body of tales until now has been marked by a broad-minded, tolerant, experimental approach, balancing the attitudes and values of one pilgrim against those of another. And though each pilgrim as teller seems to claim a certain authority for his point of view, that claim is always muted and implicit, and qualified by what follows it. The Parson's claim for authority is different: it is explicit, firm, and single-minded; it is retrospective, as we have seen, recalling the central issues of the other tales and rejecting the values of some, choosing and reinforcing the values of others; and it is followed by no qualification, but rather by authorial ratification in the Retraction. It makes an authoritative choice of one way, and is the climax of the movement toward authority that we have seen operating throughout the tales. It grants final authority in retrospect above all to those tales which have insisted on the value of patient suffering: the Knight's Tale, the Man of Law's Tale, *Melibee*, the Clerk's Tale, the Prioress's Tale, and the Second Nun's Tale. It is no accident that most of these are the very tales in which we feel least the presence of the teller; a strong personal presence would be an individuating obstacle to the authoritative message. The Parson similarly allows his material to speak for itself, as is evident if we compare his relation to the sermon material to that of the Pardoner. The Parson is willing to repeat standard moral bromides; the Pardoner manipulates them to his special purposes, and is anxious always to assert his superiority to them.

Finally, the Parson's Tale achieves authoritative closure through its relation to the Knight's Tale. I have already

167

glanced at certain topics which both tales share: bondage, and deliverance from it; "heigh estaat" and its true definition; the exercise of proper lordship; the ultimate equality in death of king and page. Both stress the value of sufferance, the pointlessness of "gruchchyng," the use of mercy. Both tales are carefully organized, and assert the order in creation: Theseus makes his "firste moevere" speech, and the Parson insists that "God hath creat alle thynges in right ordre, and no thyng withouten ordre, but alle thynges ben ordeyned and nombred" (218). In both there is a movement in the direction of reconciliation with an authoritative judge. In the Knight's Tale this is a function of the plot, and Theseus is the judge. In the Parson's Tale the movement is moral, an assertion rather than a development: on the day of doom, "biforn the seete of oure Lord Jhesu Crist," there will be "a general congregacioun, whereas no man may ben absent" (163). This judgment, together with the "supper" in heaven, hovers over the Parson's particular treatment of individual sins and sinners, providing a constant general focus: all our actions look to these final events. Above all, both tales are eschatological; both are concerned with the lack of "sikerness" in this life, and the fact that "al this thyng hath ende" (A3026). Both seek a principle of permanence in the face of these: in the Parson's Tale it is "the lyf perdurable," in the Knight's Tale it is the fact that "speces of thynges . . . / Shullen enduren by successiouns" though individuals have only "certeyne dayes and duracioun." The Knight sees the "firste moevere," that "stable is and eterne," the "propre welle" to which all things return, as the counterweight to vicissitude; one gains a stability of one's own by recognizing the larger order. The Parson's Tale ends also by defining union with the Creator in terms of recompense for vicissitude:

> Thanne shal men understonde what is the fruyt of penaunce; and, after the word of Jhesu Crist, it is the endelees blisse of hevene, ther joye hath no contrarioustee of wo ne grevaunce; ther alle harmes ben

passed of this present lyf; ther as is the sikernesse fro the
peyne of helle; ther as is the blisful compaignye that
rejoysen hem everemo, everich of otheres joye; ther as
the body of man, that whilom was foul and derk, is
moore cleer than the sonne; ther as the body, that
whilom was syk, freele, and fieble, and mortal, is inmor-
tal, and so strong and so hool that ther may no thyng
apeyren it; ther as ne is neither hunger, thurst, ne coold,
but every soule replenyssed with the sighte of the parfit
knowynge of God.   (1079)

Of course the specific nature of the recompense differs
significantly. The Knight's requires an act of the intellect, the
Parson's an act of the will. And where the Knight (or Theseus)
can speak only of the endurance of species, and a kind of
conservation of matter in the return to the "propre welle," the
Parson asserts the permanence of the individual—in company, to be sure, but in a company which preserves individual identity: "the blisful compaignye that rejoysen hem
everemo, everich of otheres joye." Thus the poem achieves
closure by offering a revised version of its first tentative
attempt at a conclusive statement; the Knight's Tale has a
"figural" relation to the Parson's Tale. The vision of the latter
fills out the vision of the former.

In sum, the Parson's Tale achieves closure by providing
various kinds of unity. It envisions community both among
men, and between men and God. It has the unifying force of
generality: it is general in a slight way in its association with
the ideas of professionalism and fitness of tale to teller, and
more deeply in its generic treatment of moral categories. This
generic treatment associates it with the General Prologue,
reconstitutes the moral categories implicit there, and places
them in a larger moral framework. It similarly places in its
large moral context most of the particular issues that arise in
the tales. But it also transcends those issues, transforming the
material of the tales into a higher spiritual plane. It replaces
the generally experiential world of the body of the poem with

its authoritative judgments, granting final authority in retrospect to the tales which have insisted on the value of patient
suffering. And finally it provides a Christian version of
Theseus's speech.

Of course the closure is not complete here; it achieves its
own fulness by being ratified by the poet's Retraction. The
Retraction is perfectly in keeping with the balance of general
and particular which the poem exhibits so consistently. One
form this takes is a pattern of return from the general to the
poet in his own person. This pattern commences in the very
opening of the poem: after the first sentence, which has
moved from the largest generalities to the relatively particular but still general statement that English pilgrims go to
Canterbury in the spring, the second sentence arrives at utter
particularity by introducing the poet:

> Bifil that in that seson on a day,
> In Southwerk at the Tabard as I lay
> Redy to wenden on my pilgrymage
> . . . .
> So hadde I spoken with hem everichon
> That I was of hir felaweshipe anon.   (A21, 32)

After describing all the pilgrims at length, he returns to
himself once more, to defend his decision to speak plainly
and to apologize for his short wit. He does the same after the
Knight's Tale, then embarks fully on the large center of the
poem, the account of the pilgrimage and the tales told on it;
and the pattern, now expanded to the full, still holds: he
returns finally to himself.[15]

But since that pattern is previously confined chiefly to the
General Prologue, the repetition of it constitutes also a kind of
reprise of the General Prologue. This is an altogether proper
mode of closure.[16] The reprise has various implications. The
poet's return to himself is made in terms of the modesty
topos, as in the General Prologue after the portraits: compare
"arrette it to the defaute of myn unkonnynge" (1082) to

Closure II: the Parson's Tale and Chaucer's Retraction

"n'arette it nat my vileynye" (A726) and "my wit is short" (A746); and "and that is myn entente" (1083) to the Miller's Prologue—itself a reprise of this topos—"Demeth nat, for Goddes love, that I seye / Of yvel entente" (A3173)[17] More significantly, we see the poet as we first saw him, joining a company, embarking on a pilgrimage: but now the company is the communion of saints, the pilgrimage is that redefined by the Parson, "thilke parfit glorious pilgrymage." The season is the season of penitence, autumnal.[18] Death, not new life, is on his mind. Here we have Chaucer's self-portrait at last, and he appears in his professional role as poet, surrounded by a list of his works. If he mentions most only to abjure them, that associates him in general with the professional virtuosity and extremism that mark the General Prologue—like many another of the pilgrims, he has misled his clientele—and in particular with the Knight, who has stripped himself of the paraphernalia of his profession in deference to the spiritual journey he is now making.

The Retraction also marks a reprise of many central elements in the tales. Christ, "of whom procedeth al wit and al goodnesse" is the One, the author of what is good in "this litel tretys" (i.e., the Parson's Tale); its faults are due to Chaucer, the representative of the many in his imperfection. Like so many of the characters in the tales, he retreats from the individual way of experience (represented by his secular poems) to the way of authority, seeking to join the company of the saved. Like the Canon's Yeoman, he has found in the return to authority a way of reaching conclusion; like the Manciple and the Parson, he speaks in favor of silence as against the mere jangling of speech. He follows the Parson also in speaking plainly, in prose, forsaking the "spiced" art of poetry. By writing in prose he also severs himself from the profession which sets him apart, and moves toward the larger company of prosaic men, in a serious and final reenactment of his move from *Thopas* to *Melibee*. This is his confession: it associates him with the Pardoner, the Wife, the Canon's Yeoman, and the Host. And although the theme of male-female opposition has no real place here, we may remind ourselves that Chaucer is one of the male pilgrims, and as such prone to go beyond common sense in his search for a spiritual ideal. Or we may see the Retraction as Chaucer's own adoption of "selinesse": he does what Melibee does, casting aside worldly prudence for radical Christian principles. To the degree that it constitutes a surprise ending, the Retraction is finally no surprise but a reinforcement of a well-established pattern in the tales, particularly the fabliaux; and as a revocation of what precedes it, it has analogues in the envoi at the end of the Clerk's Tale and the Pardoner's appeal to the pilgrims for funds. Finally, many of the tales end in a prayer for salvation, including that of the speaker; Chaucer, writing alone instead of speaking to a group, naturally enough prays at the end for his own salvation.[19] Of course, such a complex of reprises in so brief a compass is a certain reduction of many to one.

The most specific relation of all, however, is to the Parson's Tale. The language ("biwayle my giltes," "verray penitence, confessioun, and satisfaccioun," "this present lyf," etc.) is the Parson's language, the theme his theme; and like the Parson Chaucer here transforms the issues of the tales into a new spiritual plane. He rests finally in the gift of grace, in the heavenly company, and in the Trinity, praying for penitence

> thurgh the benigne grace of hym that is kyng of kynges and preest of alle preestes, that boghte us with the precious blood of his herte; so that I may been oon of hem at the day of doom that shulle be saved. *Qui cum patre et Spiritu Sancto vivit et regnat Deus per omnia secula. Amen.*

The Trinity is the only absolute marriage of one and many Chaucer knew, and the whole thrust of the poem toward balance of these terms leads inevitably to it.

Abbreviations

Baldwin	Ralph Baldwin. *The Unity of the Canterbury Tales*. Anglistica, vol. 5. Copenhagen: Rosenkilde and Bagger, 1955.
ChR	*The Chaucer Review*
David	Alfred David. *The Strumpet Muse: Art and Morals in Chaucer's Poetry*. Bloomington: Indiana University Press, 1976.
Elbow	Peter Elbow. *Oppositions in Chaucer*. Middletown, Conn.: Wesleyan University Press, 1975.
ELH	*English Literary History*
ES	*English Studies*
Howard	Donald R. Howard. *The Idea of the Canterbury Tales*. Berkeley: University of California Press, 1976.
JEGP	*Journal of English and Germanic Philology*
Justman	Stewart Justman. "Medieval Monism and Abuse of Authority in Chaucer." *ChR* 11 (1976): 95-111.
Kean	P. M. Kean. *Chaucer and the Making of English Poetry*. Vol. 2, *The Art of Narrative*. London and Boston: Routledge and Kegan Paul, 1972.
Lumiansky	R. M. Lumiansky. *Of Sondry Folk: The Dramatic Principle in the Canterbury Tales*. Austin: University of Texas Press, 1955.

MAE	*Medium AEvum*
Mann	Jill Mann. *Chaucer and Medieval Estates Satire: The Literature of Social Classes and the General Prologue to the Canterbury Tales.* London: Cambridge University Press, 1973.
MLQ	*Modern Language Quarterly*
MLR	*Modern Language Review*
MP	*Modern Philology*
MS	*Mediaeval Studies*
Muscatine	Charles Muscatine. *Chaucer and the French Tradition: A Study in Style and Meaning.* Berkeley: University of California Press, 1957.
PMLA	*Publications of the Modern Language Association of America*
PQ	*Philological Quarterly*
RES	*Review of English Studies*
Robertson	D. W. Robertson, Jr. *A Preface to Chaucer: Studies in Medieval Perspectives.* Princeton: Princeton University Press, 1962.
Robinson	F. N. Robinson, ed. *The Works of Geoffrey Chaucer.* 2d ed. Boston: Houghton Mifflin, 1957.
SP	*Studies in Philology*
UTQ	*University of Toronto Quarterly*

General Bibliographical Note

The major influence on this study has been the work of three scholars: Ralph Baldwin, Charles Muscatine, and Jill Mann. Baldwin, in *The Unity of the Canterbury Tales*, first made me (and many others) see how the poem is unified in structure. Muscatine's *Chaucer and the French Tradition* has for years been my bible for understanding Chaucer; it has certainly spurred my interest in Chaucer as a poet of relationships and syntheses. In a sense this book is an attempt to work out all the implications of Muscatine's statement that Chaucer "has a passion for relationships, and the overall structure of the work . . . meets this passion perfectly" (p. 223). Mann's *Chaucer and Medieval Estates Satire* caused me to see that one relationship in which Chaucer had an overwhelming interest was that of individual and type, or particular and general. My study was engendered in part by my attempts to work out a theoretical framework for the interest in stereotypes she documents so convincingly for the General Prologue, and to apply it to the entire poem. I have also found Donald Howard's *The Idea of the Canterbury Tales* and P. M. Kean's *Chaucer and the Making of English Poetry* stimulating and in various ways supportive. My study has intellectual affinities with two very recent works, Peter Elbow's *Oppositions in Chaucer* and Donald Rowe's *O Love! O Charite! Contraries Harmonized in Chaucer's Troilus* (Carbondale: Southern Illinois University Press, 1976), although the particular opposition I am dealing with is not germane to either. Though I am by no means a "Robertsonian," like others who would make a similar disclaimer I have learned much from D. W. Robertson's *A Preface to Chaucer;* the impulse of my argument is like his, toward unity, but I have tried to harmonize one and many rather than suppress the many in the interest of the one, as Robertson seems to me to do. The philosophical issue of one and many is well treated in A. O. Lovejoy, *The Great Chain of Being* (Cambridge, Mass.: Harvard University Press, 1936). Stephen A. Barney deals acutely and helpfully with the subject of multiplicity in the *Romance of the Rose* in the sixth chapter of his *Allegories of History, Allegories of Love* (Hamden, Conn.: Archon Books, 1979).

It was after I had completed most of my work that I came upon two articles that specifically raise the issue of one and many in Chaucer. Russell A. Peck, "Public Dreams and Private Myths: Perspective in Middle English Literature" (*PMLA* 90 [1975]: 461-67), shows briefly but provocatively how the many is related to the one in the very fundamental principles of medieval poetics. Stewart Justman, "Medieval Monism and Abuse of Authority in Chaucer" (*ChR* 11 [1976]: 95-111), shows how even the monist idea of authority is mired in multiplicity, not only in Chaucer but in the authorities themselves. Though I disagree with Justman on a number of matters (see chap. 1, n. 2), I am heartened by his essay as well as by Peck's because both support my sense that the issue of one and many is fundamentally relevant to understanding the *Canterbury Tales.* I have not seen Peck's dissertation, "Number Symbolism and the Idea of Order in the works of Geoffrey Chaucer" (Indiana University, 1962).

I have tried to read as much scholarly commentary on the poem as I could. I have purposely not made reference to much of it, however, preferring to concentrate on stating my own ideas, and wishing to avoid both the undue length and the air of contentiousness that come about when one feels obliged to work out in detail just how one's theories fit in

with, supersede, or oppose everyone else's. I trust that readers will see for themselves how my work relates to that of
others. I have, of course, acknowledged in the notes all
specific debts I was aware of, and cited adjacent but not
borrowed work when it seemed apposite to do so. I have felt
freer of the responsibility to offer constant summaries of
scholarship because of the admirable way that Howard's
recent book does that.

Notes

1. Introduction

[1]Boccaccio, in the corresponding passage in the *Teseida* (7.98), says only that "i gran baroni" (note that Chaucer's "peple" allows for greater diversity) went in groups of three, four, or six, "tra lor mostrando diverse ragioni / Di qual credevan dell' innamorati / Che rimanesse il dí vittorioso" ("trading various opinions about which of the lovers they thought would win that day"). Cf. also 7.105, where Palaemon and Arcites hear the cries "della gente mista / Che or l'uno or l'altro gien favoreggiando" ("of various people who favored one or the other"); and 8.1, of the crowd: "e qua' con questi e qua' con que' teneno" ("and some held with this one, some with that one"). Giovanni Boccaccio, *Teseida*, ed. Salvatore Battaglia (Florence: Sansoni, 1938).

On the indefinite "he" in ll. 2519-20, Robinson compares KnT A2614ff. (the account of the tournament itself).

[2]On the diversity that inheres in authority, see the important article by Stewart Justman, "Medieval Monism and Abuse of Authority in Chaucer," *ChR* 11 (1976): 95-111. This is the fullest treatment that has yet appeared of the one and the many in Chaucer. Justman argues that because there are so many contradictory authorities, and because major authorities such as Paul, Jerome, and Boethius were themselves many, authority "cannot provide what Matthew Arnold calls 'an Idea of the world' which will subdue 'the world's multitudinousness'"; "the cacophony of citations itself contributes to the impression of pluralism" (p. 96). He raises some of the same issues that are raised here, but, although I agree with him that contradictory authorities and diverse use of authority are sources of multiplicity in the poem, my conclusions are ultimately in disagreement with his. This comes about largely because various of the unifying forces which I explore are not germane to his subject, but also because, in my view, he has not attended to certain unitary aspects of the issue of

authority. Though Paul and Boethius may be forced into conceding
that the unity they seek cannot be attained, the fact that they seek it
seems to me important, as does the fact of the search for unity in
Chaucer. Paul, furthermore, can argue that diversity is good precisely because he sees that diversity as fully subsumed under God.
Nor do I accept Justman's argument that "From the emendation and
dilution of Theseus' authority in the *Knight's Tale*, to the voiding of
binding agreements and the straining and suspension of vows in the
Franklin's Tale, to the abrogation of an oath of vengeance and the
cession of authority in the *Melibee*, the tales treat of the *dis*establishment of authority" (p. 108, emphasis his). In all three of these cases
and in most other cases of such disestablishment, an inferior authority is replaced by a higher one. Theseus, for example, works
through his various mistaken authoritative judgments to a deeper
view of Providence, and Melibee's hasty oath of vengeance is
replaced by the new law of forgiveness. Nevertheless, I admire
Justman's essay, and agree fully with him on the importance of the
issue and its value as an approach to Chaucer.

[3]Robertson, pp. 367-69; cf. especially p. 369: "Chaucer tells us that the
Melibee, although it differs verbally from the other tales the audience has heard from the 'sondry folk' who proceed toward Canterbury, and contains more proverbs than any of the others, after which
it is now placed, it [*sic*] does not differ from them in *sentence*"
(emphasis his).

[4]Kean, pp. 110-11.

[5]Chaucer's *Boece*, quoted from Robinson: Book 2, prose 1; 3 pr. 2; 3 pr. 9; 3
pr. 9.

[6]Col. 1:17; the translation quoted is the Revised Standard Version.

[7]See Wayne Meeks, ed., *The Writings of St. Paul* (New York: W. W. Norton
and Co., 1972), p. 24: "Apparently certain of the Corinthian Christians regarded themselves as 'spirituals' or *perfecti* because they had
been initiated—in baptism by *their* apostle—into the sphere of
heavenly, occult 'wisdom.' They did not believe in a future 'resurrection of the dead' because they had been taught that 'in Christ' they
were already 'raised . . . up with him and enthroned with him . . . in
the heavenly places' (Eph. 2:6; cf. 2 Tim. 2:18)" (emphasis and
ellipses his). Cf. also p. 100, n.5 (to Philippians 3:15): "As in 1 Cor.,
Paul is warning against a spiritual perfectionism which regards
'resurrection' as a state already attained." See also 2 Cor. 4:7ff.; Eph.
1:10, 2, 4:12-15; Col. 3.

2. Professionalism: the Poem as Fabliau

[1]On "resoun," and the passage in general, cf. R. C. Coffin, "Chaucer and
'Resoun,'" *MLR* 21 (1926): 13-18 and Baldwin, pp. 35-37. Baldwin

defines "whiche" as "the outer man, appearance," relating profession
to "degree." I would rather regard "whiche" as equal to "what"; cf.
the Host to the Canon's Yeoman, G616: "Is he a clerk, or noon? telle
what he is." Actually, I doubt Chaucer meant each word to mean
something absolutely precise, as his concluding summary ("th'estaat,
th'array, the nombre, and eek the cause" [A716]) suggests; Baldwin's
chart of the number of "entries" for each of the original four
categories in each portrait seems quite arbitrary. I admire Baldwin's
account (pp. 35-54) of the interplay of typical and individual features
in the portraits; I think I place more emphasis on the typical,
however, and less on the individual, than he does.

²Of course the deepest rationale may be historical: Chaucer was not so
much choosing to emphasize profession as he was thinking in the
way his culture thought. That is how the Host thinks: "The devel
made a reve for to preche, / Or of a soutere a shipman or a leche"
(A3904). As Baldwin says (p. 42), in Chaucer's society "one became,
so to speak, what one did." Yet clearly there was some choice
involved on Chaucer's part; Dante, for example, places little emphasis on his characters' professions. And whatever the cause, culture or
choice, the effect is the same: the "interest" in the general is there; I
choose for rhetorical convenience to regard it as intentional.

³On the professional emphasis in the portraits, see further Mann, pp. 12-15.

⁴Baldwin and Mann are obvious exceptions, though neither carries the idea
nearly to the extent to which I shall take it in the course of this
chapter.

⁵These traits have been worked out in particular by Mann, pp. 37-54; by
Arnold Williams, "Chaucer and the Friars," *Speculum* 28 (1953):
499-513 and "The 'Limitour' of Chaucer's Time and his 'Lim-
itacioun,'" *SP* 57 (1960): 463-78; and by Penn R. Szittya, "The Friar as
False Apostle: Antithetical Exegesis and the *Summoner's Tale,*" *SP* 71
(1974): 19-46.

⁶The clerk in the Franklin's Tale is not himself a lover, but arranges (as far
as he is asked) for a successful outcome of Aurelius's suit; clearly he
could do the same for himself if he wanted to.

⁷Of these, the Miller's, Reeve's, and Friar's Tales have the fullest portraits;
the Cook's Tale also has a full portrait of Perkyn. The portraits of the
merchant, wife, and monk in the Shipman's Tale are all quite brief;
the "portrait" of the friar in the Summoner's Tale is given in terms of
his actions on the day of the tale. My remarks on fabliaux are derived
strictly from Chaucer's practice as exhibited in these six tales, and do
not apply to the entire genre. As Muscatine and others have shown, in
the French fabliaux traits of character tend to be introduced singly,
as needed for the plot, rather than in a formal portrait. On fabliau
portraits, see J. L. Lowes, *Geoffrey Chaucer* (Oxford: Clarendon
Press, 1934), pp. 176-80; Louis A. Haselmeyer, "The Portraits in

Chaucer's Fabliaux," *RES* 14 (1938): 310-14; and Muscatine, chapters 1, 2, and 6. On the fabliau in general, cf. especially D. S. Brewer, "The Fabliaux," in *Companion to Chaucer Studies*, ed. Beryl Rowland, rev. ed. (New York and Oxford: Oxford University Press, 1979), pp. 296-325; Per Nykrog, *Les Fabliaux*, rev. ed. (Geneva: Droz, 1973); Jean Rychner, *Contribution à l'étude des fabliaux*, 2 vols. (Geneva: Droz, 1960); and the recent, very sensible work of Glending Olson, "The Medieval Theory of Literature for Refreshment and its Use in the Fabliau Tradition," *SP* 71 (1974): 291-313, and "The *Reeve's Tale* as a Fabliau," *MLQ* 35 (1974): 219-30. Olson offers a corrective to heavily moralistic readings of Chaucer's tales, and stresses the contest of trickery in the Reeve's Tale. He does not relate it to the notion of "tricks of the trade," however, and in general it seems to me that the professional emphasis in Chaucer's fabliaux has not been attended to. (I have not seen Olson's dissertation, "The Cultural Context of Chaucer's Fabliaux," Stanford, 1968.)

[8]By a higher generalization, "clerks" and "monks" are both "clerics," schooled churchmen. Thus though the Monk and the Clerk in the General Prologue differ widely, the monk in the Shipman's Tale can play the same role as the students in the Miller's Tale and the Reeve's Tale. The merchant in the Shipman's Tale is not said specifically to be old, but the monk, who is thirty, is said to be young (B1216, 1218), and both he and the wife are clearly younger than the merchant.

[9]My notion that the descriptive technique of the General Prologue may derive in part from the fabliaux can, I think, coexist with J. V. Cunningham's telling account of its relation to the dream vision in "The Literary Form of the Prologue to the *Canterbury Tales*," *MP* 49 (1952): 172-81, reprinted with the title "Convention as structure: the Prologue to the *Canterbury Tales*" in his *Tradition and Poetic Structure* (Denver: Alan Swallow, 1960), pp. 59-75. But surely its major relation is to estates satire, as Mann has amply shown.

[10]Lumiansky (p. 237) calls this trio "a tightly knit group of city businessmen." See also his article, "Chaucer's Cook-Host Relationship," *MS* 17 (1955): 208-9.

[11]If one speculates what it is about fabliaux that causes this professional interest, several answers suggest themselves. The fabliau is a bourgeois form. It depends on a practical joke, and these are likely to arise out of professional traits or situations, or to be seen as having some special ironic appropriateness to certain professions (e.g. the fart is an ironic symbol of the friar's hypocrisy; the devil as agent of Satan reflects ironically on the summoner's relation to his archdeacon). The joke needs a certain specificity of character in order to give it point, but it cannot afford either the space or the psychological interest and sympathy of deep characterization; professional stereotypes mediate nicely between the extremes to be avoided.

[12] The Pardoner's Tale has been associated with the fabliaux, on quite different grounds from those presented here, by Nancy H. Owen, "The Pardoner's Introduction, Prologue, and Tale: Sermon and Fabliau," *JEGP* 66 (1967):541-49. She argues cogently that the conflict between the Host and Pardoner follows the fabliau patterns of victimization by sexual jest and of subsequent quite unsympathetic treatment of the victim.

[13] The implications of treating womanhood or wifehood as a profession are developed further in the next chapter. The idea was familiar in estates satire. Ruth Mohl reports that some estates writers put women in with each estate or profession; "the general practice, however, is to ignore the matter of estate so far as women are concerned and treat them all as women. Their estate seems not to matter so much as the fact that they are women, with duties and defections peculiar to themselves." (*The Three Estates in Medieval and Renaissance Literature* [New York: Columbia University Press, 1933], pp. 20-21). Similarly, Mann, p. 121: "the first question that confronts us is what estate the Wife of Bath represents—and the answer is not far to seek, for women were recognized as a separate class in estates lists"; and H. S. V. Jones, "The Plan of the 'Canterbury Tales,'" *MP* 13 (1915): 45-48: "Particularly interesting as anticipating the Wife of Bath, who alone among Chaucer's pilgrims is not introduced specifically as the representative of a calling, is the recognition of matrimony as one of the *états*" (i.e., she *is* introduced by her calling) (p. 46). See further Robert P. Miller, "The Miller's Tale as Complaint," *ChR* 5 (1970): 147-60.

[14] "Dame" here might mean a friend such as her "gossyb dame Alys" (D548), rather than her mother. But cf. the tavern boy in the Pardoner's Tale, "Thus taughte me my dame" (C684), and especially the Manciple: "thus taughte me my dame: / 'My sone . . .'" (H318).

[15] On women as scholars, see also MerchT, E1428. The trope is in Jean de Meun: see Muscatine, pp. 93 and 95, and his further references to the tradition of *la vieille qui enseigne*, p. 260, n. 57.

[16] "A leef" D635, but "thre leves" D790.

[17] The idea that the Pardoner intends his collection from the beginning is not new. It is explored most fully by Lumiansky, pp. 202-22. For further references, and for a summary of various opinions on the Pardoner, see John Halverson, "Chaucer's Pardoner and the Progress of Criticism," *ChR* 4 (1970): 194-202. Howard's subtle account of the Pardoner in his final chapter is very fine; although he explicitly rejects Lumiansky's notion of the Pardoner's plan (p. 346, n. 17), his emphasis on the Pardoner's "method," his "tricks," his "art" seems not inconsistent with mine. I too see him as a man "willing to take extravagant gambles and having an overpowering lust to win, or an unconscious will to lose, or a taste for danger" (p. 353). But my main

purpose is simply to show how the Pardoner shares in the general professionalism of the poem.

[18]The Pardoner's professionalism has many analogues in the Canon's Yeoman's Prologue and Tale, treated fully in chapter 6 below. The Yeoman says his Canon is "to wys," has "over-greet a wit," so that what he does is "overdoon" (G644-48). One of the experimenters after the explosion insists that, like merchants, "Us moste putte oure good in aventure" (G946). It is in the nature of money-making to risk your capital, as the Pardoner in effect does. Finally, the canon in the Yeoman's tale ropes his victims in by first seeming to reveal his tricks (G1123-39).

[19]From another point of view, we can see the Friar's Tale as toying with the truism that the victim must be someone wholly different from the practitioner. Once the summoner realizes that his traveling companion is a fellow agent, he abandons any thought he might have had of victimizing him. But the fiend is able to victimize the summoner despite their professional similarity—which goes to show what a very stupid summoner he is.

[20]In *Sir Thopas* we not only have a caricature of the "profession" of knight-errantry, its accoutrements and conventions, we also have Chaucer showing off in a special way his own skill as a poet—and he is embarrassed (if unfairly) for it. Of course he is showing off his skill everywhere; he is like the Parson in that he enacts his trade directly rather than speaking about it. The Pardoner and the Canon also try to ply their trade, and the Wife is evidently on the pilgrimage to find a sixth husband. We have, indeed, in these an interesting group of "busman's holidayers," pilgrims for whom the pilgrimage is "ernest" in a professional sense.

3. Men and Women and Marriage

[1]In order to avoid endless repetition of phrases like "in Chaucer's view" or "the poem implies," I have frequently throughout this chapter simply stated, as I have in this sentence, what I think the poem says about male and female roles, without saying explicitly that the poem says it. Such statements should not be misunderstood as my own views on men and women.

[2]For further comment on the opposition between the Parson and the Wife, see chapter 7, especially pp. 158-59. A subtle instance occurs when the Parson quotes Saint Paul writing to Timothy, reproving those who "weyven soothfastnesse, / And tellen fables and swich wrecchednesse" (ParsProl, I34): Paul warns specifically against old wives' tales *(aniles fabulas)*, 1 Tim. 4:7.

[3]An ancient and enduring notion: cf. Proverbs 31:13, 19, 21, 22, 24; the jingle

"When Adam delved and Eve span, / Who was then the gentleman?"; and the curious persistence of the phrase "the distaff side." Cf. also the Pardoner's "Cometh up, ye wyves, offreth of youre wolle" (C910), and Goodelief Bailly's "I wol have thy knyf, / And thou shalt have my distaf and go spynne," as reported by her husband (B3097).

[4]A rough count yields seventy-eight men, thirty-one women, or a ratio of two-and-one-half to one. Only WBT has more major female characters than male, and then only if we count Guenevere but not Arthur as major. PardT and CYT have no female characters at all. The occasional female protagonists (Constance, Virginia, Grisilde, Dorigen, Cecilia) are all doing lonely battle in a world of men. They stand out more in their tales than men do in theirs precisely because of the male emphasis of the poem, and its assumption that women are interesting *as women*.

[5]The Man of Law's ironic "housbondes been alle goode" (B272) is negligible, since removing the irony yields, not "all husbands are bad" but only "not all husbands are good." The Reeve generalizes about *old* men in his prologue. In the tercelet's statement in the Squire's Tale that "men loven of propre kynde newefangelnesse" (F610), it is quite baffling to decide whether "men" means "males" or "human beings." The analogue to the passage in MancT is of little help because of its irony.

[6]This passage is quoted by Robertson, p. 269, to illustrate his contention that "characters in Chaucer's narrative tend to react in accordance with their moral natures rather than in accordance with their natures as free psychological entities in a world of free events." This is a good statement of Chaucer's resistance to particularity; but I would want to substitute "sexual or professional" for "moral," or at least to argue that most of his characters' "moral natures" are determined by sex or profession or both.

[7]Symkyn in the Reeve's Tale is a little like Chauntecleer (or the Nuns' Priest or Solomon), a single male in a house full of females: his wife, his daughter, his mares. The male clerks invade this harem from the male world of Cambridge, with a male horse. As in NPT, the women become pawns in the "professional" conflict among the males.

[8]But immediately after this he accepts the notion that Satan knows "the olde wey" to women, and makes them his instruments. This perhaps excuses women by making Satan the culprit for their wickedness— but it accepts the wickedness.

[9]Chaucer preserves this twoness by not providing a portrait of the Second Nun; he would also have been hard put to make one, since the portrait of the Prioress has taken care of this one non-wifely female profession. A further hint that he did not or could not differentiate

the two nuns is the fact that both utter Dante's prayer of praise to Mary (B474-80, G50-56). The division of women into wicked wives and saints is, of course, hardly confined to Chaucer. See Hope Phyllis Weissman, "Antifeminism and Chaucer's Characterizations of Women," in *Geoffrey Chaucer*, ed. George D. Economou (New York: McGraw Hill, 1975), 93-110. She isolates Eve and Mary as prototypes. See also Francis L. Utley, *The Crooked Rib* (Columbus: Ohio State University Press, 1944). He distinguishes two complementary genres of literature on women, satire and defense, clearly corresponding to the two views. Eighty-five of the 403 pieces he lists are defenses of women. As Utley shows on pp. 7-9, the paired attitudes have always existed side by side in Western culture.

[10]Of course I recognize that these sexual stereotypes are hardly confined to the Canterbury Tales, but are a staple of comic tradition. Orgon and Elmire in Molière's *Tartuffe* are a good example; and an excellent example from medieval comedy (alluded to in MillT) is Noah's wife balking at entering the ark: contemptuous of her husband's silly scheme, she wants to keep her feet on the ground.

[11]The basic pattern for the male-female contrast is, of course, Adam and Eve. The original fabliau is Genesis 3, in which an apparently preoccupied Adam allows the clever intruder Satan to usurp his power over his wife, and Eve talks Adam into doing what she wants him to do. This pair hovers behind the treatment of men and women in the poem: in the "man's confusion" lines cited above; in the plot and scenery (yard or garden) of NPT, FranklT, MerchT; in several explicit allusions to Adam or Eve or both, not only in NPT and MerchT, but also in MLT, Mel, PardT, WBP, and ParsT; in the account of them which opens MkT; in the comparison, explicit in January's case and implicit in others, of marriage to paradise, and the concomitant wry suggestion that marriage is purgatory, as it is for the Wife's fourth husband (D489), or hell, as it is for May (E1964). Pertelote provides Chauntecleer with both bliss and *confusio*, and would like to provide him with purgation as well.

[12]   Pacience is an heigh vertu, certeyn,
    For it venquysseth, as thise clerkes seyn,
    Thynges that rigour sholde nevere atteyne.   (FranklT, F775)

[13]Perhaps the ultimate vindication of women's practical sense is that they generally manage to live longer than their men, as Criseyde does. As the Merchant says, "A wyf wol laste, and in thy hous endure, / Wel lenger than thee list, paraventure" (E1318). The Wife, as usual, is the best example: she has outlived five husbands. Emily outlives Arcite, Constance outlives Alla, the mother in the Prioress's Tale lives on to lament her son (who is a small version of the typically obsessed male). In the Monk's Tale, Samson is survived by Delilah, Hercules by Deianira, and Croesus by his daughter; Zenobia, the Monk's one

tragic heroine, is still alive at the end of his account of her, as few of his heroes are. Cecilia dies last, preceded by Valerian, Tiburce, and Maximus. On the other hand, Virginia is killed by her father, and Phebus kills his wife.

[14]Or he may be substituting authority for his own experience altogether, since his own experience bears out neither his praise of men nor his dispraise of women: Proserpine seems in fact to be true to him, and he himself is a rapist.

[15]"Visaging" is a good example of the way the sexual stereotyping is always open to ironic undercutting by the notion of professionalism: merchants must also "make chiere and good visage," as the merchant in the Shipman's Tale explains to his wife (B1420)—a lesson she and other women take to heart in their own commerce.

[16]Cf. WBP, D402: "Deceite, wepyng, spynnyng God hath yive / To wommen kyndely." Deceit here specifically includes swearing (D397) and chiding (D408, 419), and "continuel murmur or grucchyng" (D406) as well. Utley (*Crooked Rib*, pp. 180-81) quotes a Latin source and an English analogue, and, on pp. 3-4, a Latin couplet which adds lying and not keeping silence.

[17]Some other exponents of "suffisant answere" are the old woman in the Friar's Tale, who finds the words to overcome the summoner; Grisilde in her marvelously effective speech to Walter as she leaves to return to her cottage; Cecilia in her answer to Almachius; Prudence. Cecilia's and Prudence's apparent "male" learning is perhaps less central than the persuasive boldness it gives them. Alison's "Tehee!" is quite sufficient, and together with Nicholas she bears down John before the townspeople.

[18]A fondness for generality, that is, a resistance to "propriety," may explain Chaucer's willingness to repeat proper names, like John for a priest, or Alice, which the Wife shares not only with Alison in MillT but with her "gossyb dame Alys" (D548).

[19]Again I speak of the values of the poem; cf. ParsT I923 (the man is the "heved"), 930 (the wife should be "subget"); also 260ff. (reason should rule over sensuality) and 325ff. (Adam represents reason, Eve delight of the flesh), and Saint Paul's injunction to wives to submit to their husbands (Eph. 5:22). For an extensive analysis of all that Theseus's conquering of "the regne of Femenye" may have meant, see Richard L. Hoffman, "The Canterbury Tales," in R. M. Lumiansky and Herschel Baker, eds., *Critical Approaches to Six Major English Works* (Philadelphia: University of Pennsylvania Press, 1968), pp. 61-70. For the application of the passages in the Parson's Tale to marriage, see Robert Scholes and Robert Kellogg, *The Nature of Narrative* (New York: Oxford University Press, 1966), pp. 94-95; see also Robertson, pp. 317-31.

[20]For a representative listing, see Gerhard Joseph, "*The Franklin's Tale: Chaucer's Theodicy,*" *ChR* 1 (1966): 21, n. 2. To my mind the most thorough and persuasive attack on the old view is Alan T. Gaylord, "The Promises in *The Franklin's Tale*," *ELH* 31 (1964): 331-65. For a brief but trenchant assessment, see John L. Hodge, "The Marriage Group: Precarious Equilibrium," *ES* 46 (1965): 289-300, especially pp. 295-99.

[21]I do not mean to imply here that all opposition to clerks is female. John the Carpenter and Symkyn despise them, and even the Nuns' Priest (since he cannot "bulte" predestination "to the bren" [B4430]) and the Parson ("I putte it ay under correcioun / Of clerkes, for I am nat textuel" [I57]) disclaim clerkliness. But the Nuns' Priest and the Parson are merely using the modesty topos; female opposition seems far less respectful.

4. Experience and Authority

[1]The theme of experience and authority is familiar enough in Chaucer criticism, but to my mind it has never been explored, at least before Justman, with the fulness it deserves. Robertson treats it implicitly by taking the medieval authorities with deadly seriousness, and in general giving short shrift to what is "experiential" in the poem. The theme is treated occasionally by many critics—e.g. Howard, pp. 297-98 and elsewhere; Muscatine, pp. 204ff. (vis-a-vis the Wife), Elbow, pp. 95ff. Arthur Hoffman's stimulating essay, "Chaucer's Prologue to Pilgrimage: the Two Voices" (*ELH* 21 [1954]: 1-16), is also relevant, since the "nature" and "supernature" he finds balanced in the General Prologue correspond, roughly and in part, to experience and authority, and to many and one. Alfred David treats it at a number of places in *The Strumpet Muse* (Bloomington: University of Indiana Press, 1976)—see his index, s.v. "experience"—and explores the issue in the Wife's Prologue in full detail. The major treatment is in Robert O. Payne's *The Key of Remembrance* (New Haven: Yale University Press, 1963), in which Chaucer's esthetic is defined as an attempt to balance the conflicting demands of experience, books (tradition, authority), and "ideal knowledge" (as represented by dreams and visions in the early poems). Though Payne does not employ this idea in any specific way in his chapter on the *Canterbury Tales*, he draws convincingly on a number of passages from that poem about artistic values as he explores the basis of Chaucer's esthetic in his second chapter. What I hope to add to all this is both a much more detailed exploration of the issue, and a demonstration of how it fits the larger idea of the relation of one to many.

[2]For other treatments, see David, pp. 135-58, and Payne, *The Key of Remembrance*, pp. 66-67. I have also said enough about the Friar's and Summoner's Tales in chapter 2 to leave them out here. Both

continue the Wife's concern with authority, or "scole-matere," as the Friar calls it (D1272). The summoner in the Friar's Tale is a parody of the searcher for knowledge in his "evere enqueryng upon every thyng" (D1409); the devil teaches him a lot about hell, but looks forward to the time when the summoner's direct experience of hell will enable him to speak of it *ex cathedra;* he will be a greater authority on hell than Vergil or Dante (D1517-20) or a "maister of dyvynytee" (D1636-38). The Tartuffian friar in the Summoner's Tale is acutely conscious of his master's degree; one of the funniest lines in this brilliant tale is his attempt to extract a donation from Thomas with the threat "Or elles mote we oure bookes selle" (D2108)—as if Thomas cared. The friar's bogus authority is set against not only genuine authority figures like the Parson, the lord and lady at the end of the tale, and Saints Francis and Dominic, but also against the common sense derived from experience of ordinary people like Thomas. Thomas, who has been to the school of hard knocks, sets a "probleme," a "question" (D2219, 2223) to the friar, which baffles him, but for which the lord's squire Jankyn provides a "demonstracion," speaking "subtiltee" as well as Euclid or Ptolemy (D2224, 2290). Thomas and Jankyn are finally the best scholars in the tale. The fart satirizes preaching in the same way that Chauntecleer's "chuk" or the inarticulate cries of both humans and animals in the chase scene in NPT satirize Chauntecleer's ample rhetoric.

[3]Egeus's counterpart among the gods is Saturn, who "knew so manye of aventures olde" that he "foond in his olde experience an art / That he ful soone hath plesed every part" (A2446). Though he pleases "every part," he is like Egeus in being ultimately partial himself.

[4]*Chaucer's Poetry: An Anthology for the Modern Reader,* 2d ed. (New York: Ronald Press, 1975), p. 1043.

[5]For a somewhat different treatment of the Knight's Tale which also lays emphasis on what Theseus learns, see Georgia Ronan Crampton, *The Condition of Creatures: Suffering and Action in Chaucer and Spenser* (New Haven: Yale University Press, 1974), pp. 49-75. I have also been stimulated by P. M. Kean's profound understanding of the Knight's Tale, which appears not only in her chapter on it, but throughout her treatment of the *Canterbury Tales.*

[6]The fabliaux may appear "experiential" in that they ignore ordinary canons of morality, the ten commandments, for instance. But they substitute for it a perceptual morality, whose virtues are intelligence and common sense, which has an even greater authority than ordinary moral canons because it is less controversial. One may argue whether adultery is a sin, but no one will deny the value of knowing oneself and how one should act.

[7]R. W. Babcock, "The Mediaeval Setting of the 'Monk's Tale,'" (*PMLA* 46 [1931]: 205-13) distinguishes between a clerical tradition of "tragic"

tales, which was moralistic, and a non-clerical tradition, which was not. He places the Monk's performance firmly in the latter group; to my mind the evidence suggests rather that Chaucer interwove the two traditions.

[8]An especially interesting generalization, since, ironically, one only comes to realize the truth of it if it is disobeyed. (Of course we needn't all disobey it; only Chauntecleer need do so. We can then read about him in a book.) Chauntecleer would not in fact have undergone a "dreadful" experience if he had not ignored the dream; the dream can only come true if he ignores it. The tale seems to imply that dreams are to dread only if you don't dread them. It is as if authority relies on being ignored; if it weren't ignored it wouldn't be authority. But further, Chauntecleer finds the words to avoid being eaten. Ultimately the experience is not dreadful: the experience is that it was all right to ignore the dream.

[9]At another level, the separate characters of cock, hen, and fox do not matter. The story says that everybody is a fool: all three characters are outwitted. This takes it beyond the fabliaux, in which usually someone emerges as clearly superior, as well as beyond the Monk's Tale: the Monk sometimes stresses pride, sometimes the animosity of others, as the cause of one's downfall; the Nuns' Priest shows both operating simultaneously.

5. Closure

[1]E.g. by Edward S. Cohen, "The Sequence of the Canterbury Tales," *ChR* 9 (1974): 190-95, or by John H. Fisher, ed., *The Complete Poetry and Prose of Geoffrey Chaucer* (New York: Holt, Rinehart and Winston, 1977), p. 2, and many others. Actually, discussion of the number of tales per pilgrim is rare; most references to the issue are, like Cohen's, *obiter dicta* in essays on the order of the tales, and most critics simply assume that Chaucer reduced his plan but never got around to changing the Host's proposal in the General Prologue. The only critic known to me who has given the problem full attention is Charles A. Owen, Jr. in various articles and, most fully, in his recent book, *Pilgrimage and Storytelling in the Canterbury Tales* (Norman: University of Oklahoma Press, 1977), which lists the earlier articles on p. 220, n. 1. Owen adduces more evidence than anyone else for the discrepancy between "one tale," "one or two tales," and "four tales," but ignores much of what is given here; and he concludes idiosyncratically that the change was in the direction of one to four: Chaucer began intending one tale per pilgrim, then expanded to four. This theory, first offered in 1951, has won little acceptance; it relies on so complex an argument, and on a conception of the poem so diametrically opposite to mine, that I see little point in attempting to refute it in detail.

²In presenting the evidence I follow the "Bradshaw order" of Pratt's edition; but my argument in no way depends on that order.

³Of course there is no guarantee that the rubrics are authorial, and in fact they vary considerably from manuscript to manuscript, as a glance at Sir William McCormick's *The Manuscripts of Chaucer's Canterbury Tales* (Oxford: Clarendon Press, 1933) will show. See also J. M. Manly and Edith Rickert, *The Text of the Canterbury Tales*, 8 vols. (Chicago: University of Chicago Press, 1940), 3:528-32; they find the rubrics "only slightly traditional" (p. 531). However, virtually all the manuscripts have rubrics, and those in Ellesmere, which Pratt prints and to which I refer, are typical (but a number of manuscripts have rubrics in Latin, which reveal less than English rubrics: "fabula militis" can mean "a tale by the Knight," not necessarily "the Knight's tale"). One indication (apart from one's knowledge of medieval practice) that rubrication, if not authorial, must have occurred early in the tradition is the fact that WBP and PhysT, since they have no introduction, rely on the rubric for initial identification, and the Second Nun is identified as the teller of her tale only in the rubrics: there is no introduction, and the transition to CYT is made in the line "Whan ended was the lyf of Seinte Cecile" (G554), with no reference to the teller.

⁴The Knight makes several further references to the need for economy by employing the figure of *occupatio;* cf. A1188, 1190, 1380, 2206-7, 2965-66. Cf. also the Host's reminders of the passing of time and the need for haste: to the Reeve (A3899ff.), to the company in general before calling on the Man of Law (B16ff.), and to the Parson (I70).

⁵Though in general the argument of this study implies limits to the dramatic theory, I do not by any means wish to abandon it altogether. The evidence that the Shipman's Tale was once assigned to the Wife further supports my argument here: I take it that, having hit on the idea of her Prologue and Tale, Chaucer saw that it would be undermined if she also told the Shipman's Tale; he found that he could not use tales to characterize tellers if they told more than one. It is common to complain that Boccaccio's tellers are far blander than Chaucer's; but it is precisely because they each tell ten tales that he cannot characterize them through their tales.

⁶Perhaps he has not mentioned the Nuns' Priest in the General Prologue at all, since the phrase "and preestes thre" (A164, not printed by Pratt; see his note there) may be scribal.

⁷The Monk, however, does say "or ellis, first, tragedies wol I telle" (B3161); see below.

⁸Conceivably "this day" implies that the Man of Law expects to tell further tales on subsequent days; but I take the phrase rather to refer to his return to the present moment and its demands after his digression on Chaucer.

[9]Cf. "a yeer or two" (A1381, 1426, F574); "a day or two" (A3668, B1005, 3643, 4151, E2404, F1348); "a furlong wey or two" (A4199, B557, E516); "a word or two" (C630, F701); "a pound or two" (G674); "o mawmet or two" (I749); "lecchours oon or two" (D1325); etc. (However, the phrase "seven yeer" in KnT A1452 means that "a yeer or two" in ll. 1381 and 1426 must mean "two" in both cases, since the only other addendum in the total of seven is "thre yeer" 1446; these calculations of time are not in Boccaccio.) And with the Monk's "a tale, or two, or three" (B3158) and the Summoner's "tales two or thre" (D846), cf. "a yeer, or two, or thre" (B4246); "prestes two or thre" (C371); "two yeer or thre" (F1582); "a noble, or two, or thre" (G1037); and "ounces two or three" (G1104). Since "a tale" can mean "anything told," perhaps especially a bit of gossip, we can consider the Summoner to have told a number of things on friars, and the Monk to have fulfilled amply the plurality of "a tale, or two, or three" by telling seventeen.

[10]On the Summoner, see also the previous note. In Owen's opinion, the Host's interruptions of Chaucer and the Monk argue a one-tale plan: his offers to them of another chance "make no sense if each pilgrim will have by right three more turns in the competition" (*Pilgrimage and Storytelling*, p. 17). For the question whether the Cook expects several chances, see the Appendix to this chapter.

[11]The fact that Chaucer never completed that tale seems irrelevant, since the unfinished tale of the Squire "counts" for him, as the words of the Franklin indicate. Actually, the surprising invitation to the Cook may be accounted for if we suppose an agreement among the pilgrims that anyone caught napping must tell a tale as his "forfeit." Several things suggest this, chiefly the Host's "do hym come forth, he knoweth his penaunce" (H12). He has never commanded a tale, only requested one, and he has never used the word "penaunce" (which Chaucer uses to mean "suffering," or "satisfaction for sin," or occasionally "punishment for sin") to refer to one's duty to fulfil the "forward." Conceivably it refers to the penalty for disobeying the Host, to pay "al that we spende by the weye" (A806): "he knows the penalty for refusing me." But if it means that, the phrasing is unusually telescoped; the Host seems to refer to some actual, not potential, transgression. Furthermore, the Manciple suggests, successfully, that the Cook be excused; his present drunken stupor would not seem an adequate reason for releasing him altogether from the basic obligation to tell a tale, but it would be enough to excuse him from a penalty tale such as I have supposed. Chaucer may have intended to establish such a penalty at some point, or he may have regarded the word "penaunce" as a sufficient stage direction in itself. However, even if this is the explanation for the invitation to the Cook, it still serves to open a new possibility for extension. Of course it is also possible that Chaucer meant to cancel the present Cook's Tale from Group A, as W. W. Skeat thought (*The Complete Works of Geoffrey Chaucer*, 6 vols. [Oxford: Clarendon

Press, 1900], 3:399). Or it is possible that the fragmentary tale we have was originally placed here, but then moved back to what Frederick Tupper calls "the more congenial neighborhood" of MillT and RvT ("Chaucer and the Seven Deadly Sins," *PMLA* 29 [1914]: 114); but if Chaucer did that, he did not make the necessary adjustment here. I should admit that working against this suggestion of mine—which I offer diffidently—is the fact that when the Host tells the Monk that were it not for the Monk's clinking bells, "I sholde er this han fallen doun for sleep," he mentions no such consequence, but only that the Monk's Tale "hadde . . . be toold in veyn" (B3989).

[12]Chicago: University of Chicago Press, 1968.

[13]Since we already have a carpenter in the Reeve, and since the other four artisans are in textile trades, I wonder if "carpenter" is a scribal error—for cordwainer (shoemaker), perhaps, or clothier, or clothmaker.

[14]Some have thought that the Franklin interrupts the Squire; but my point is the same in either case. Two small but curious instances of Chaucer's freedom with numbers, one an addition, one a diminishment, occur in the Wife's Prologue and the Pardoner's Tale. At D667 the Wife says she tore "a leef" from the Book of Wykked Wifes; at D790 she says "thre leves." The youngest rioter in the Pardoner's Tale, at C872, fills two bottles with poison; but at C886 his companions take "the botel ther the poyson was." Theseus's speech at the end of the Knight's Tale, which seems so generally relevant, fits the pattern of diminishment in the tales nicely: created things cannot outlive their allotted days, "al mowe they yet tho dayes abregge" (A2999). The poem is "abridged" from the Host's hopeful plan as Arcite's life is abridged. KnT, MillT, and RvT all emphasize how plans go awry, and so do the links. The harmony of the General Prologue is to the conflicts in the links as the neatness of the Host's plan is to its later breakdown.

[15]Gerhard Joseph, "Chaucerian 'Game'—'Earnest' and the 'Argument of Herbergage' in the *Canterbury Tales*," *ChR* 5 (1970): 93-94 makes a similar point. Chaucer, he says, in the General Prologue is "caught up in the ample sense of time and space that the comfortable 'herberwes' of this world encourage"; but by the Parson's Prologue this plan "has been seriously constrained by the exigencies of time."

[16]Since Baldwin's pioneering work, with his clear demonstration of how the pilgrimage works as a symbol, few scholars have found it useful to hold on to the old positivistic postulate of a return journey. I see no value in it. On the failure to reach Canterbury, Baldwin says, "The destination of the pilgrimage becomes, by the interlocked metaphorical and dramatic structure, not so much the Canterbury shrine as the Parson's Tale, because it unfolds the *wey* to Him who is the way, the truth, and the light" (pp. 92-93). And again, "It is in the nature of the construct that the Parson conclude the tales of a journey

whose destination becomes thereby neither Southwerk nor Canterbury, but the Holy City of Jerusalem" (p. 84). The most cogent modern adherent of the theory that some tales are told on the return journey is Charles Owen; see *Pilgrimage and Storytelling*, pp. 10-47. But I think Owen simply misses Chaucer's point that the return trip doesn't matter, only the "parfit glorious pilgrymage" matters. In the Parson's Prologue, as David nicely says, "We do not know how many days the pilgrims have been travelling or whether they are still on the way to Canterbury or on the way home, and we do not need to know. Placing the two passages [ML Prol and Pars Prol] side by side, we get the feeling of having lived through a long and satisfying day" (p. 131). See also Howard, p. 72, where he shows that the one-way journey is "endemic to the idea of a pilgrimage," a fact borne out in pilgrimage narratives and voyage literature, in which the homecoming is not important.

6. Experience and Authority II: The Canon's Yeoman's Tale

[1]For a thorough analysis of how CYT is related to SNT, see Bruce A. Rosenberg, "The Contrary Tales of the Second Nun and the Canon's Yeoman," *ChR* 2 (1968):278-91.

[2]E.g. Rosenberg, ibid., p. 282; R. G. Baldwin, "The Yeoman's Canons: A Conjecture," *JEGP* 61 (1962): 232-43. John Gardner, "*The Canon's Yeoman's Prologue and Tale:* An Interpretation" (*PQ* 46 [1967]: 1-17), maintains the distinction, and essentially agrees with me when he says that the Canon "is probably a charlatan, but he is also a passionate believer in his art" (p. 8). Muscatine (p. 216) expresses the distinction nicely: "The chantry priest is swindled by the alchemist in the second part just as the alchemist is swindled by the science in the first." However, though my reading of the tale owes much to Muscatine's, I find the Canon's relation to the science not wholly a matter of being swindled.

[3]The two parts of the tale stand in a relation to each other similar to that of the Wife's prologue and tale, a relation that can generally be called one of experience and authority. The second part is "authoritative" in several ways: though presented as true, it is fictive or authorial in its purposeful plot structure (a trick planned and successfully executed), in its not involving the teller as a character (if it is true, the Yeoman can only have heard it, and so is telling it on the authority of another), in its use of stereotypes of the professional confidence man and the sucker he tricks, in the way it serves a series of morals. It lends authority to the Yeoman's new realization that alchemy is a deceptive game. The first part is obviously experiential in contrast, since it gives a disordered account of personal experience. It has, to be sure, its elements of authority, above all because like the Wife's prologue it is an account of an art, and like hers it has its ironies; but its experiential side dominates, as my account of it indicates.

4"Swindling Alchemist, Antichrist," *Centennial Review* 6 (1962): 569.

5In Boethian terms, the Canon seeks downward what he should seek upward; cf. the numerous images of mining in the meters of the *Consolation of Philosophy,* and especially Book 3, meter 8: "Folk . . . ploungen hem in erthe, and seken there thilke good that surmounteth the hevene that bereth the sterris"; and Orpheus, in Book 3, meter 12, who represents whoever may "ficche his eien into the put of helle," losing "the noble good celestial." For an enlightening Boethian reading of the entire tale, see Bruce L. Grenberg, "The *Canon's Yeoman's Tale:* Boethian Wisdom and the Alchemists," *ChR* 1 (1966): 37-54.

6The movement of the Canon's Yeoman's Prologue and Tale thus matches the movement of the entire poem, which also comes to rest in authority; see chapter 7. I am not worried, as many are, by the apparent dramatic inappropriateness of what seems a new level here of alchemical knowledge on the Yeoman's part. As Muscatine sensibly says, "the characterization of the speaker is suspended in favor of comment on the wider meaning of his position" (p. 215). The move in the direction of authority carries all before it, including any concern—if Chaucer had it—for realism or consistency of character.

7 "Labor lost" is an insistent motif in the poem: beside the Pardoner's revelers is the Pardoner himself, whose endeavors to win money from the pilgrims fail; beside Arcite is the parodic Absolon, laboring in vain to win Alison. Cf. also John's work in preparation for the flood, Aurelius's to move the rocks, the summoner's work in FrT and the friar's work in SummT. The professional emphasis of the poem serves not only to define stereotypes; it also makes for an inevitable concern with work, and for a certain elegiac tone when work is wasted. Every profession involves an alchemy of a sort, an attempt at transformation, and often the transformation hoped for does not come about. The Parson puts the issue in terms of "good works," of "quickening" and "mortifying," and says "wel may that man that no good werk ne dooth synge thilke newe Frensshe song, '*Jay tout perdu mon temps et mon labour*'" (I248); see below, pp. 164-65.

8Cf. also ParsT, I777-80, on "deceite bitwixe marchaunt and marchant," the "marchandise that men haunten with fraude and trecherie and deceite, with lesynges and false othes," which is "cursed and dampnable." Merchandise always suggests falsity in Chaucer.

9The lapse is due in part simply to the Yeoman's desire to bring this part of his narrative to a close. As against the inconclusiveness of the Canon's experiments, he finds a tidy way to stop. This may suggest that the generalizing tendency in the poem is at least in part a function of its nature as a poem: narrative poetry has an inner drive toward conclusiveness that makes it inevitable that a teller such as the Yeoman will find some effective way of dealing with experiences which before were fragmented and inconclusive. That is, it is the act of telling his tale which enables him to reach conclusion, just as the Wife comes in the course of her Prologue to understand herself. His "conversion experience" is made up in part of his association with the company of pilgrims—his joining of a community of ordinary people, while the Canon departs—but in part of giving a narrative account of his life and art which forces him to impose a general meaning on them. This process has an important bearing on the Retraction and the whole process of closure treated in chapters 5 and 7: one feels that Chaucer, too, like his characters, is forced by the act of telling his poem to move toward some all-embracing conclusion. This need not have been the Retraction, perhaps, but the breadth of experience covered in the poem could hardly sustain a conclusion less broad. (Paradoxically, the poem is also an experience of failing to reach conclusion: in SqT, CkT, in the failure to provide tales for the Yeoman, the Guildsmen, the Plowman, in the foreshortening of the Host's plan. This experience we have as readers of a failure to reach the object of desire is a powerful ingredient in forcing us to generalize failure; and when we do we are forced to realize that the Canon's experience is not fully particular. It follows a general pattern of desire and failure.)

[10]This point is not particularly new; I think no one has ever read the CYT without feeling the sense of ending. Rosenberg (in "Swindling Alchemist, Antichrist" pp. 575-78) puts the solemn spiritual issues, and the sense of ending, persuasively in the form of the threat of Antichrist at the end of the world. Gardner, in showing that alchemists who have severed themselves "from al that evere they hadde" for their art are like the man in Christ's parable who sells all for "the pearl of price, joy hereafter" ("*The Canon's Yeoman's Prologue and Tale*," p. 12), and in associating Arnold of Villa Nova with the New Jerusalem, likewise implies that the Parson's vision of joy in heaven is appropriately near at hand. See also Howard, p. 297; Muscatine, pp. 220-21.

[11]On this point, and the way it introduces ParsT and the Retraction, see Wayne Shumaker, "Chaucer's Manciple's Tale as Part of a Literary Group," *UTQ* 22 (1953): 147-56; see also Howard, pp. 298-306.

7. Closure II: the Parson's Tale and Chaucer's Retraction

[1]In a more general way, one might compare its normative function to Hrothgar's sermon in *Beowulf;* to Trevrizent's discourses in *Parzival*, or Vergil's and Beatrice's in *The Divine Comedy;* and perhaps to Anchises' long prophetic and explanatory speech in Book 6 of the *Aeneid*. And one might think of Proverbs or Ecclesiastes as well as Revelation. Chaucer, in short, had ample precedent for mixing overt morality with narrative.

[2]Compare these lines, with their repeated "o," to SNT 207-8 (quoted above, p. 125). Brotherhood is a motif in the General Prologue: cf. the Parson and Plowman, the "greet fraternitee" to which the Guildsmen belong, and the Friar, who debases brotherhood; see also Palamon's and Arcite's oath of brotherhood (broken, like that of the Pardoner's three rioters); the further treatment of friars in SummT; Justinus and Placebo, who offer, respectively, true and false brotherhood to January; Cambalo and Algarsyf, Valerian and Tiburce.

[3]For a fuller treatment of this important theme, cf. Gerald J. Schiffhorst, ed., *The Triumph of Patience: Medieval and Renaissance Studies* (Orlando: University Presses of Florida, 1978).

[4]This is, of course, the message of *Melibee*.

[5]Cf. 1255ff., 455, 499ff., 654-76, 729ff., 831, 861, 925ff., 1053-56.

[6]Of course the Parson fails to catch the holiday mood.

[7]John Finlayson, "The Satiric Mode and the *Parson's Tale*" (*ChR* 6 [1971]: 94-116), treats the fitness of the tale to the Parson in quite a different way; he suggests—somewhat diffidently—that its various harsh ideas constitute a certain satiric exposé of the Parson's shortcomings. I find his argument even less convincing than he does.

[8]Cf. the General Prologue, A377, 449-52; and 1407.

[9]Frederick Tupper, in "Chaucer and the Seven Deadly Sins" (*PMLA* 29 [1914]:93-128), tried to argue that this concept was the key to the design of the poem. He is not convincing, however, as J. L. Lowes shows in detail in an essay of the same title in *PMLA* 30 (1915): 237-371. Tupper continued to press his theory in "Chaucer's Sinners and Sins," *JEGP* 15 (1916): 56-106.

[10]See WBP, D697ff., on "the children . . . of Venus"; cf. also Pratt's illustration and note, pp. 270-71, and Kean, p. 25.

[11]Many are noted in Kate O. Peterson, *The Sources of the Parson's Tale* (Boston: Ginn and Co., 1901); and in Emil Koeppel, "Über das Verhältnis von Chaucers Prosawerken und die Echtheit der 'Parson's Tale,'" *Archiv für das Studium der neueren Sprachen und Literaturen* 87 (1891): 33-54. See also Robinson's notes. As Paul Ruggiers says, "Many a student has discovered from examining the catalog of sins that many passages afford a commentary upon certain of the pilgrims and upon certain ideas which bind the stories together"; but Ruggiers doubts that one can see "in anything but a general sense that the tales have their final commentary in the various parts of the sermon." (*The Art of the Canterbury Tales* [Madison: University of Wisconsin Press, 1967], pp. 251-52.) See also a similar brief dismissal of the matter in Howard, pp. 377-78. I have tried to grant a specific sense to the notion Ruggiers raises. My attempt is more complete than Baldwin's (pp. 101-4). I also think that Baldwin misjudges the

parallels by applying the dramatic theory too literally: he imagines the Wife as the "target" of the Parson's comments on lechery, wonders whether the Pardoner "could . . . have been unmoved by the return of his text," and so on. There seems little point in imagining the pilgrims as listening to the Parson's Tale. Baldwin saw that Canterbury disappears as the object of pilgrimage, being replaced by the City of God. He seems not to have seen that this pilgrimage and these individual pilgrims also disappear.

[12] Two interesting essays on the Parson's Prologue are Russell A. Peck, "Number Symbolism in the Prologue to Chaucer's *Parson's Tale*" (*ES* 48 [1967]: 205-15), and Rodney Delasanta, "The Theme of Judgment in *The Canterbury Tales*" (*MLQ* 31 [1970]: 298-307). Both emphasize the sense of ending, and the transformation to spiritual values, Peck through a rather intricate set of meanings attached to numbers, Delasanta by making clear the eschatalogical emphasis. Both also emphasize the image of the feast, though Peck's assertion that "presumably, after the sun has set . . . the . . . pilgrims . . . will arrive at Canterbury, go to confession where they will tell the tale which will win for them the Lord's Supper, that is, the Eucharist which they will take on Easter morning" (p. 209) seems merely to replace the old positivism of the return journey with a new positivism of too precise allegorical correspondences.

[13] E.g. KnT, MLT, MkT, ClT, WBP, WBT, FrT, SNT, CYT, FranklT, MerchT, SqT, MancT. On the whole subject of thraldom, see Stephen A. Barney, "Troilus Bound," *Speculum* 47 (1972):445-58.

[14] See Delasanta, "The Theme of Judgment."

[15] Of course the account of the pilgrimage is not without several other such returns: the references in MLT to Chaucer's works; the exchanges with the Host over *Thopas;* and the beginning of the Canon's Yeoman's and Parson's prologues. But in all these we see Chaucer briefly as pilgrim, or as teller of his own two tales, not as author of the entire text. The Retraction is the first time since the Miller's Prologue that Chaucer has returned to his authorial self.

[16] Cf. Barbara Herrnstein Smith, *Poetic Closure* (Chicago: University of Chicago Press, 1968), pp. 27, 66-67.

[17] Olive Sayce, "Chaucer's 'Retractions': the Conclusion of the *Canterbury Tales* and its Place in Literary Tradition" (*MAE* 40 [1971]: 230-48), similarly associates the topos of retraction with the larger topos of modesty. My association of the Retraction with the General Prologue should be seen in the context of her demonstration that the Retraction contains a number of motifs that commonly appear at the beginning or the end of medieval religious poems. On page 241, she includes the word *entente* in a list of terms which recur frequently in the examples she has studied.

[18]The Parson's emphasis on fruit is implicitly autumnal; in the sentence "for in the flour is hope of fruyt in tyme comynge, and in foryifnesse of synnes hope of grace wel to do" (288), he makes an explicit seasonal analogy. In general the "flour" and literal springtime of the General Prologue have been replaced by the "fruyt" and autumnal atmosphere of the Parson's Tale, just as the sunrise near the end of the General Prologue is replaced by the slanting afternoon sun of the Parson's Prologue.

[19]This is, of course, one of the motifs of ending, as Sayce ("Chaucer's 'Retractions'") has shown.

Index

Adam and Eve, 61, 70-71, 77, 101, 161, 186, 187
Alain de Lille, 27
Alchemists, standard traits of, 129
Alchemy, 127, 132, 135, 137, 141, 144, 164-66
Augustine, Saint, *Confessions*, 120
Authority, 23, 68, 83-108 passim; contradictions in, 17, 85-86, 179-80. *See also* Experience and Authority
"Aventure," 140-42

Babcock, R. W., 189-90
Bailly, Herry. *See* Host
Balance, 71; between continuation and closure, 120; between experience and authority, 144; in FranklT, 80; in Gen Prol, 112; in KnT, 94; between one and many, 13-31 passim, 64, 72; between portrait and narrative, 127; and Retraction, 170
Baldwin, R. G., 194
Baldwin, Ralph, 175, 180-81, 193-94, 197-98

Barney, Stephen A., 176, 198
"Becoming," 119-20
Beowulf, 196
Bible, 105-6, 163; form of, and form of *CT*, 147, 162, 196; gospels, 22; Job 10:20-22, quoted in ParsT, 156-57; Proverbs, 184. *See also* Paul, Saint
Boccaccio, 179, 191
Boethius, *Consolation of Philosophy*, 27-28, 102, 119-20, 179-80, 195
"Bradshaw order," 108, 191
Brewer, D. S., 182
Brotherhood, 197
"Busman's holidayers," 184

Canon, 18, 45, 118, 131-32, 134
Canon's Yeoman, 51, 85, 125-46, 171; words of Host to, 110, 115
Canon's Yeoman's Tale, 62, 125-46; and alchemy, 14; and "craft," 140-42; diverse opinions in, 12-13, 14; and experience/authority, 84, 102, 194; explosion scene in, 45, 128, 137-44; and fabliaux, 44-45; and

MerchT, 144-45; and ParsT,
164-66; and professionalism,
184; rhythm of expansion
and contraction in, 138; and
"tricks of the trade," 42,
128-30
Canterbury, arrival at, not
reported, 109, 119
Canterbury Tales: form of
whole, 15, 26, 27, 30, 39-42,
92, 101-2, 159, 167-69; related
to form of Bible, 147, 162,
196; "fragmentary" status
of, 30
Chaucer, Geoffrey: and
failure to reach conclusion,
137; as pilgrim, 109, 116, 118,
198; and Retraction, 170-72;
selectivity of, 118-19; and
Thop, 184
Christianity, 28-30, 102-8
Clerk, 34, 36, 38, 40, 62-63;
words of Host to, 114
Clerks: generic traits, 38,
84-85, 182; opposed to
women, 40, 43, 44, 63, 76,
154, 188
Clerk's Tale: "envoi," 172;
experience/authority in,
83-84; "gathering"
convention in, 20; men and
women in, 26, 59, 60, 65,
70, 72, 73, 74, 187; and
ParsT, 160, 161; "patient
suffraunce" in, 167;
thraldom in, 166; unity in,
18, 24, 26
Closure, 109-21, 167-72; and
CYT, 145-46; forces
working against, 117; and
MancT, 146; and movement
toward goal, 119; and
narrative, 195-96; and

"pattern of diminishment,"
117-18; reader's expectation
of, 116-17
Clothing, 15, 34-35, 126, 127,
156-57, 158
Coffin, R. C., 180
Cohen, Edward L., 190
Confession, 48-51, 146; by
Canon's Yeoman, 132-46;
and Retraction, 171
Confidence game, in CYT,
130-31
Convention, 20, 30, 37, 46
Conversion: of Canon's
Yeoman, 132-33; and goal of
pilgrimage, 145
Cook, 34, 36, 40, 118, 123-24,
192-93
Cook's Tale, 42, 62, 72, 119,
160
"Craft," 140-42
Crampton, Georgia Ronan,
189
Cunningham, J. V., 182

Dante, 181, 186, 189, 196
David, Alfred, 188, 194
Delasanta, Rodney, 198
Diminishment, 136-37
Diversity: balanced with
unity, 13-14; emphasized by
sexual differences, 71-72; of
opinions on women, 63;
various examples, 12-14. *See
also* Generality;
Multiplicity; One and
Many; Unity
Doctor. *See* Physician
Donaldson, E. T., 94

Elbow, Peter, 175-76
Experience, 68, 131, 132, 140
Experience and Authority,
83-108, 188; in CYT, 125-48,

194; and closure, 120; in
FrT, 188-89; and "goal" of
poem, 119; in KnT, 86-95;
and marriage, 71-72; in *Mel*,
102-8; in MkT, 96-97; in
NPT, 97-101; in ParsT,
167-68; in SecNT, 125; in
SumT, 188-89; in WBP, 44.
See also Authority

Fabliaux, 181-82; vs. beast
fable, 98; climactic scenes
in, 45; compulsive boasting
in,49-50; and FranklT, 78;
and Gen Prol portraits, 39;
and genre of *CT*, 39-42, 101;
morality in, 189; and NPT,
190; portraits in, 127, 181-82;
"professional" retribution
in, 142; professionalism in,
39-42; and Retraction, 172;
various conventions, 46
Finlayson, John, 197
Fisher, John H., 190
Food, 157, 159, 163
Fortune, 96-97, 140
Franklin, 40, 158; words of
Host to, 110, 115, 116
Franklin's Tale: authority in,
180; clerk in, 38; marriage
in, 74-80; men and women
in, 60, 62, 72; movement
toward unity in, 24; and
number of tales, 113; and
ParsT, 160, 161; thraldom in,
166
Freedom (and thraldom),
151-52, 163, 165-67, 168, 198
Friar: and generic traits of
friars, 36-37; and number of
tales, 116; and Parson, 154,
155; and ParsT, 158, 161; and
professionalism, 35, 39, 40
Friar's Tale: and confession,

49, 51; experience/authority
in, 188-89; lack of
generalizations on women
in, 62; and multiplicity, 18;
and ParsT 160, 161; portrait
of summoner in, 37; and
professionalism, 46, 47, 184;
retribution in, 142; "suffisant
answere" in, 187; and "tricks
of the trade," 41
Friendship, 149-50, 157

Gardner, John, 194, 196
Gaylord, Alan T., 188
General Prologue, 70, 92,
101-2, 154, 166, 180-81;
"artificial" harmony in, 26,
119; and Canon and
Yeoman, 126; and closure,
117, 118; and "gathering"
passage in KnT, 18-21;
general categories in, 33-35;
and number of tales per
pilgrim, 109, 110, 112; and
ParsT, 92, 101-2, 148, 154-59,
162, 164; portraits in, 36
(Friar), 37 (Summoner),
55-58 (Wife and Parson),
94-95 (Knight and Squire),
154-56 (Parson); portraits in,
and "diminishment," 118;
portraits in, and fabliaux,
39; portraits in, and
portraits in tales, 36-39;
professional emphasis in,
35-36; and Retraction,
170-71; trust in professional
skill in, undermined in tales,
142; unifying categories in,
15; waning of dominance
of, 145; women in, 64
Generality: and categories in
Gen Prol, 34-35; in form of
CT, 15; in Gen Prol, 15;

Index

46-47, 146, 172; compared to
Canon, 131; and confession,
51, 171; and Host, 40, 41, 47;
and multiplicity, 18; and
Parson, 154, 155, 167; and
professionalism, 40, 41, 43,
45, 46-47, 52; and
Retraction, 171, 172
Pardoner's Tale: and CYT,
137; and experience/
authority, 84, 102-3; and
men and women, 61; and
ParsT, 160, 161; and
professionalism, 42, 44-45,
46-47; retribution in, 142
Parson: and Friar, 155; and
Host, 109-10, 114, 115, 116;
and knowledge, 69; and
Pardoner, 155, 167; portrait
of, 34, 36, 55-58, 69, 154-56;
and professionalism, 40-41,
155-56; and Retraction, 171;
and Wife of Bath, 55-58,
154, 158-59
Parson's Prologue, 109-10, 115,
116, 119, 146, 162-63
Parson's Tale, 30; and CYT,
164-66; and closure, 146;
description of contents,
148-53; and form of CT, 92,
102, 107-8; and Gen Prol, 92,
102, 154-59; and "goal" of
CT, 193-94; and Mel, 107-8;
and men and women, 59,
62, 187; movement toward
unity in, 24; and
professionalism, 40-41, 52,
153-54; "transformation" in,
149, 162-67, 172; unity in,
153; wisdom of, 85
Particularity, in CYT, 130. See
also Generality
Parzival (Wolfram von
Eschenbach), 196

"Patient suffraunce," 66,
152-53, 159, 161, 167, 168, 186
Pattern of diminishment,
117-21, 193
Paul, Saint, 17-18, 27, 28-30,
71, 79, 105, 106, 179-80, 184
Payne, Robert O., 188
Peck, Russell A., 176, 198
Peterson, Kate O., 197
Physician, 40
Physician's Tale, 62, 85, 111,
113, 160, 164
Plato, 27
Plowman, 109
Portraits: and authority/
experience, 127; in fabliaux,
39, 81-82. See also General
Prologue; names of
individual pilgrims
Pratt, R. A., 10, 191, 197
Prioress, 40
Prioress's Tale, 62, 105, 167
Professionalism, 30, 33-53;
animosity based on, 39-41,
123; and authority, 84-85; in
CYT, 125-46 passim, 184;
and craft, 141; and exposure
of fraud, 48-51; and
fabliaux, 39-42, 142, 182;
and FranklT, 76, 78; and
FrT, 184; and Gen Prol, 15,
35-36; and men and
women, 40, 42-46, 55, 57-64,
71, 183, 187; and MillT, 95;
and NPT, 66; and ParsT,
153-54, 155-56; and
Retraction, 171; summary,
52-53; in SumT, 36-37; and
Thop, 184; and "tricks of
the trade," 36, 41-47, 128-29;
and work in CT, 195
Proverbs, 22, 84-85, 95, 100,
103, 133, 143-44

207